COWLES FOUNDATION

for Research in Economics at Yale University

Monograph 12

COWLES FOUNDATION

For Research in Economics at Yale University

SECOND EDITION

Social Choice
and
Individual Values

Kenneth J. Arrow

New Haven and London, Yale University Press

Copyright, 1951 © 1963 by Cowles Foundation for
Research in Economics at Yale University.
Sixth printing, 1973.
Originally published by John Wiley & Sons, Inc.

International standard book number: 0–300–01363–9 (cloth),
0–300–01364–7 (paper)
Printed in the United States of America by
The Murray Printing Company,
Forge Village, Massachusetts.

Published in Great Britain, Europe, and Africa by
Yale University Press, Ltd., London.
Distributed in Latin America by Kaiman & Polon,
Inc., New York City; in Australasia and Southeast
Asia by John Wiley & Sons Australasia Pty. Ltd.,
Sydney; in India by UBS Publishers' Distributors Pvt.,
Ltd., Delhi; in Japan by John Weatherhill, Inc., Tokyo.

To Selma, my wife

PREFACE TO SECOND EDITION

The literature on the theory of social choice has grown considerably beyond the few items in existence at the time the first edition of this book appeared in 1951. Some of the new literature has dealt with the technical, mathematical aspects, more with the interpretive. My own thinking has also evolved somewhat, although I remain far from satisfied with present formulations. The exhaustion of the first edition provides a convenient time for a selective and personal stocktaking in the form of an appended commentary entitled, "Notes on the Theory of Social Choice, 1963," containing reflections on the text and its omissions and on some of the more recent literature. This form has seemed more appropriate than a revision of the original text, which has to some extent acquired a life of its own.

K. J. A.

Tokyo, Japan
August 1963

ACKNOWLEDGMENTS

FIRST EDITION

This study was initiated in the summer of 1948 while I was on leave from the Cowles Commission as a consultant to The RAND Corporation, which is engaged in research under contract with the United States Air Force. It was further developed and assumed its present form at the Cowles Commission during the period of October, 1948, to June, 1949, as part of the general research program of the Commission which is conducted under a grant from the Rockefeller Foundation. During part of this period support was also received from The RAND Corporation under a contract between RAND and the Cowles Commission for the study of resource allocation. To these organizations I wish to express my appreciation for the interest shown in this study and for the facilities accorded to me.

I wish to express my indebtedness to the following individuals at RAND: A. Kaplan, University of California at Los Angeles, and J. W. T. Youngs, University of Indiana, for guidance in formulating the problem, and D. Blackwell, Howard University, and O. Helmer for other helpful discussions. The manuscript has been read by A. Bergson and A. G. Hart, Columbia University, and by T. C. Koopmans, Cowles Commission for Research in Economics and the University of Chicago, and I owe much, both in improvement of presentation and in clarification of meaning, to their comments. Development of the economic implications of the mathematical results has been aided by the comments of F. Modigliani, Cowles Commission and the University of Illinois, T. W. Schultz, University of Chicago, and H. Simon, Cowles Commission and Carnegie Institute of Technology. I have had the benefit of comments by J. Marschak, Cowles Commission and the University of Chicago, on the question of the measurability of utility, touched on in Chapter II. The section in Chapter VII on the decision process as a value in itself has benefited from suggestions by P. J. Bjerve, Central Statistical Bureau, Oslo, Norway, then a guest of the Cowles Commission, and M. Friedman, University of Chicago. For guidance in the unfamiliar realms of political philosophy, I must thank D. Easton, University of Chicago. The mathematical exposition has been considerably improved as a result of comments by T. W. Anderson, Cowles Commission and Columbia University, E. Nagel, also of Columbia University, J. C. C. McKinsey, The RAND Corporation, and J. W. T.

Youngs. I must also mention the stimulation afforded by several staff meetings of the Cowles Commission in which my thesis was submitted to the research group for discussion and criticism. Needless to say, any error or opacity remaining is my responsibility.

I cannot fully acknowledge here the great debt I owe to my many teachers, but I cannot refrain from singling out H. Hotelling, now of the University of North Carolina, to whom I owe my interest in economics and particularly my interest in the problems of social welfare.

Acknowledgment is also due Mrs. Jane Novick, Editorial Secretary of the Cowles Commission, for preparing the manuscript for publication and seeing it through the press and to Miss Jean Curtis, Editorial Assistant, for valuable aid in proofreading and preparation of the index.

Second Edition

I wish to thank Miss Laura Staggers, of the Stanford Institute for Mathematical Studies in the Social Sciences, for her patient typing and retyping of the manuscript for Chapter VIII.

K. J. A.

CONTENTS

CHAPTER I

INTRODUCTION

1. THE TYPES OF SOCIAL CHOICE

In a capitalist democracy there are essentially two methods by which social choices can be made: voting, typically used to make "political" decisions, and the market mechanism, typically used to make "economic" decisions. In the emerging democracies with mixed economic systems, Great Britain, France, and Scandinavia, the same two modes of making social choices prevail, though more scope is given to the method of voting and decisions based directly or indirectly on it and less to the rule of the price mechanism. Elsewhere in the world, and even in smaller social units within the democracies, social decisions are sometimes made by single individuals or small groups and sometimes (more and more rarely in this modern world) by a widely encompassing set of traditional rules for making the social choice in any given situation, e.g., a religious code.[1]

---

[1] The last two methods of making social choices are in a sense extreme opposites, developments of conflicting tendencies in a democracy. The rule of the single individual is the extreme of administrative discretion, the rule of a sacred code the extreme of rule by law. But in dynamic situations the rule of a sacred code leads by insensible steps to dictatorship. The code needs interpretation, for conditions change, and, no matter how explicit the code may have been in the first place in determining how society shall act in different circumstances, its meaning becomes ambiguous with the passage of time. It might conceivably happen that the job of interpretation passes to society as a whole, acting through some democratic process—"vox populi, vox dei." Or it can happen that interpretation passes to the hands of the people individually and not collectively; in this case, as soon as differences of opinion arise, the religious code loses all its force as a guide to social action. See, for example, the ultimate consequences in the field of economic ethics of the Protestant insistence on the right of each individual to interpret the Bible himself (R. H. Tawney, *Religion and the Rise of Capitalism*, London: J. Murray, 1926, pp. 97–100). But more likely, in view of the authoritarian character of the sacred code, the interpretation will pass into the hands of a single individual or a small group alone deemed qualified.

The classification of methods of social choice given here corresponds to Professor Knight's distinction among custom, authority, and consensus, except that I have subdivided consensus into the two categories of voting and the market (F. H. Knight, "Human Nature and World Democracy," in *Freedom and Reform*, New York: Harper and Bros., 1947, pp. 308–310).

The last two methods of social choice, dictatorship and convention, have in their formal structure a certain definiteness absent from voting or the market mechanism. In ideal dictatorship there is but one will involved in choice, in an ideal society ruled by convention there is but the divine will or perhaps, by assumption, a common will of all individuals concerning social decisions, so in either case no conflict of individual wills is involved.[2] The methods of voting and the market, on the other hand, are methods of amalgamating the tastes of many individuals in the making of social choices. The methods of dictatorship and convention are, or can be, rational in the sense that any individual can be rational in his choices. Can such consistency be attributed to collective modes of choice, where the wills of many people are involved?

It should be emphasized here that the present study is concerned only with the formal aspects of the above question. That is, we ask if it is formally possible to construct a procedure for passing from a set of known individual tastes to a pattern of social decision-making, the procedure in question being required to satisfy certain natural conditions. An illustration of the problem is the following well-known "paradox of voting." Suppose there is a community consisting of three voters, and this community must choose among three alternative modes of social action (e.g., disarmament, cold war, or hot war). It is expected that choices of this type have to be made repeatedly, but sometimes not all of the three alternatives will be available. In analogy with the usual utility analysis of the individual consumer under conditions of constant wants and variable price-income situations, rational behavior on the part of the community would mean that the community orders the three alternatives according to its collective preferences once for all, and then chooses in any given case that alternative among those actually available which stands highest on this list. A natural way of arriving at the collective preference scale would be to say that one alternative is preferred to another if a majority of the community prefer the first

---

[2] It is assumed, of course, that the dictator, like the usual economic man, can always make a decision when confronted with a range of alternatives and that he will make the same decision each time he is faced with the same range of alternatives. The ability to make consistent decisions is one of the symptoms of an integrated personality. When we pass to social decision methods involving many individuals (voting or the market), the problem of arriving at consistent decisions might analogously be referred to as that of the existence of an integrated society. Whether or not this psychiatric analogy is useful remains to be seen. The formal existence of methods of aggregating individual choices, the problem posed in this study, is certainly a necessary condition for an integrated society in the above sense; but whether the existence of such methods is sufficient or even forms an important part of the sufficient condition for integration is dubious.

alternative to the second, i.e., would choose the first over the second if those were the only two alternatives. Let A, B, and C be the three alternatives, and 1, 2, and 3 the three individuals. Suppose individual 1 prefers A to B and B to C (and therefore A to C), individual 2 prefers B to C and C to A (and therefore B to A), and individual 3 prefers C to A and A to B (and therefore C to B). Then a majority prefer A to B, and a majority prefer B to C. We may therefore say that the community prefers A to B and B to C. If the community is to be regarded as behaving rationally, we are forced to say that A is preferred to C. But in fact a majority of the community prefer C to A.[3] So the method just outlined for passing from individual to collective tastes fails to satisfy the condition of rationality, as we ordinarily understand it. Can we find other methods of aggregating individual tastes which imply rational behavior on the part of the community and which will be satisfactory in other ways?[4]

If we continue the traditional identification of rationality with maximization of some sort (to be discussed at greater length below), then the problem of achieving a social maximum derived from individual desires is precisely the problem which has been central to the field of welfare economics. There is no need to review the history of this subject in detail.[5] There has been controversy as to whether or not the econo-

[3] It may be added that the method of decision sketched above is essentially that used in deliberative bodies, where a whole range of alternatives usually comes up for decision in the form of successive pair-wise comparisons. The phenomenon described in the text can be seen in a pure form in the disposition of the proposals before recent Congresses for federal aid to state education, the three alternatives being no federal aid, federal aid to public schools only, and federal aid to both public and parochial schools. The "paradox of voting" seems to have been first pointed out by E. J. Nanson (*Transactions and Proceedings of the Royal Society of Victoria*, Vol. 19, 1882, pp. 197–240). I am indebted for this reference to C. P. Wright, University of New Brunswick.

[4] The problem of collective rationality has been discussed by Knight, but chiefly in terms of the socio-psychological prerequisites. See "The Planful Act: The Possibilities and Limitations of Collective Rationality," in *Freedom and Reform, op. cit.*, pp. 335–369, especially pp. 346–365.

[5] Good sketches will be found in P. A. Samuelson's *Foundations of Economic Analysis*, Cambridge, Massachusetts: Harvard University Press, 1947, Chapter VIII; and A. Bergson (Burk), "A Reformulation of Certain Aspects of Welfare Economics," *Quarterly Journal of Economics*, Vol. 52, February, 1938, pp. 310–334. A summary of recent developments will be found in the article, "Socialist Economics," by A. Bergson, in *A Survey of Contemporary Economics*, H. S. Ellis, ed., Philadelphia: The Blakiston Co., 1948, Chapter XII. In addition to the above, restatements of the present state of the field will be found in O. Lange, "The Foundations of Welfare Economics," *Econometrica*, Vol. 10, July–October, 1942, pp. 215–228; and M. W. Reder, *Studies in the Theory of Welfare Economics*, New York: Columbia University Press, 1947, Chapters I–V.

mist *qua* economist could make statements saying that one social state is better than another. If we admit meaning to interpersonal comparisons of utility, then presumably we could order social states according to the sum of the utilities of individuals under each, and this is the solution of Jeremy Bentham, accepted by Edgeworth and Marshall.[6] Even in this case we have a choice of different mathematical forms of the social utility function in terms of individual utilities; thus, the social utility might be the sum of the individual utilities or their product or the product of their logarithms or the sum of their products taken two at a time. So, as Professor Bergson has pointed out, there are value judgments implicit even at this level.[7] The case is clearly much worse if we deny the possibility of making interpersonal comparisons of utility. It was on the latter grounds that Professor Robbins so strongly attacked the concept that economists could make any policy recommendations,[8] at least without losing their status as economists and passing over into the realm of ethics. On the other hand, Mr. Kaldor and, following him, Professor Hicks have argued that there is a meaningful sense in which we can say that one state is better than another from an economic point of view,[9] even without assuming the reality of interpersonal comparison of utilities. The particular mechanism by which they propose to accomplish the comparison of different social states, the compensation principle, will be examined in more detail in Chapter IV.

The controversy involves a certain confusion between two levels of argument. There can be no doubt that, even if interpersonal comparison is assumed, a value judgment is implied in any given way of making social choices based on individual utilities; so much Bergson has shown clearly. But, given these basic value judgments as to the mode of aggregating individual desires, the economist should investigate those

[6] F. Y. Edgeworth, *Mathematical Psychics*, London: C. Kegan Paul and Co., 1881, pp. 56–82, especially p. 57; "The Pure Theory of Taxation," in *Papers Relating to Political Economy*, London: Macmillan and Co., 1925, Vol. II, pp. 63–125, especially pp. 100–122. The interpretation of social utility as the sum of individual utilities is implicit in Marshall's use of the doctrine of consumers' surplus, though other assumptions are also involved. (A. Marshall, *Principles of Economics*, New York: The Macmillan Co., eighth edition, 1949, pp. 130–134, 467–476.)

[7] Bergson, "A Reformulation . . . ," *op. cit., passim.* See also Samuelson, *op. cit.*, pp. 219–252.

[8] L. Robbins, *An Essay on the Nature and Significance of Economic Science*, second edition, London: Macmillan and Co., 1935, Chapter VI; "Interpersonal Comparisons of Utility: A Comment," *Economic Journal*, Vol. 43, December, 1938, pp. 635–641.

[9] N. Kaldor, "Welfare Propositions of Economics and Interpersonal Comparisons of Utility," *Economic Journal*, Vol. 49, September, 1939, pp. 549–552; J. R. Hicks, "The Foundations of Welfare Economics," *Economic Journal*, Vol. 49, December, 1939, pp. 696–700, 711–712.

mechanisms for social choice which satisfy the value judgments and should check their consequences to see if still other value judgments might be violated. In particular, he should ask the question whether or not the value judgments are consistent with each other, i.e., do there exist any mechanisms of social choice which will in fact satisfy the value judgments made? For example, in the voting paradox discussed above, if the method of majority choice is regarded as itself a value judgment, then we are forced to the conclusion that the value judgment in question, applied to the particular situation indicated, is self-contradictory.

In the matter of consistency, the question of interpersonal comparison of utilities becomes important. Bergson considers it possible to establish an ordering of social states which is based on indifference maps of individuals, and Samuelson has agreed.[10] On the other hand, Professor Lange, in his discussion of the social welfare function, has assumed the interpersonal measurability of utility,[11] and elsewhere he has insisted on the absolute necessity of measurable utility for normative social judgments.[12] Professor Lerner similarly has assumed the meaningfulness of an interpersonal comparison of intensities of utility in his recent work on welfare economics.[13]

In the following discussion of the consistency of various value judgments as to the mode of social choice, the distinction between voting and the market mechanism will be disregarded, both being regarded as special cases of the more general category of collective social choice. The analogy between economic choice and political choice has been pointed out a number of times. For example, Professor Zassenhaus considered the structure of a planned economy by considering the free market replaced by influence conceived generally as a means of distributing the social product.[14] He argued that, under conditions analogous to free competition, the market for exchanging influence for goods would come to equilibrium in a manner analogous to that of the ordinary market, political influence taking the place of initial distribution of goods. His model, however, is expressed only in very general terms, and it is not easy to see how it would operate in a socialist democracy, for example.

[10] See the discussion of the Fundamental Value Propositions of Individual Preference in Bergson, "A Reformulation . . . ," *op. cit.*, pp. 318–320; Samuelson, *op. cit.*, p. 228.

[11] Lange, *op. cit.*, pp. 219–224, especially top of p. 222; but there are contradictory statements on p. 223 and at the top of p. 224.

[12] O. Lange, "The Determinateness of the Utility Function," *Review of Economic Studies*, Vol. 1, June, 1934, pp. 224–225.

[13] A. P. Lerner, *Economics of Control*, New York: The Macmillan Co., 1944, Chapter III.

[14] H. Zassenhaus, "Über die ökonomische Theorie der Planwirtschaft," *Zeitschrift für Nationalökonomie*, Vol. 5, 1934, pp. 507–532.

Dr. Howard Bowen has considered voting as the demand for collective consumption.[15] In his treatment he regards distribution of income and costs as given, and other simplifying assumptions are made. Close analogies are found with the ordinary market demand curve.

Knight has also stressed the analogy between voting and the market in that both involve collective choice among a limited range of alternatives.[16] He has also stressed certain differences, particularly that there is likely to be a greater tendency toward inequality under voting than under the market; these differences are, however, largely of a sociopsychological type rather than of the formal type which alone is relevant here.

More recently, there has been a series of papers by Professor Duncan Black, dealing with various aspects of the theory of political choice under certain special assumptions and emphasizing the close similarity between the problems of market and electoral choice.[17] His work will be dealt with in greater detail in Chapter VII, Section 2. There is also a literature on the technical problems of election. The chief relevant point here is that virtually every particular scheme proposed for election from single-member constituencies has been shown to have certain arbitrary features. The problem of choosing by election one among a number of candidates for a single position, such as the Presidency of the United States or membership in a legislative body when each district returns only a single member, is clearly of the same character as choosing one out of a number of alternative social policies; indeed, selection among candidates is presumably a device for achieving selection among policies.

2. SOME LIMITATIONS OF THE ANALYSIS

It has been stated above that the present study confines itself to the formal aspects of collective social choice. The aspects not discussed may be conveniently described as the game aspects, especially since that term has acquired a double meaning. In the first place, no con-

[15] H. R. Bowen, "The Interpretation of Voting in the Allocation of Economic Resources," *Quarterly Journal of Economics*, Vol. 58, November, 1943, pp. 27–48.

[16] F. H. Knight, "Economic Theory and Nationalism," in *The Ethics of Competition and Other Essays*, New York: Harper and Bros., 1931, pp. 294–305.

[17] D. Black, "On the Rationale of Group Decision-Making," *Journal of Political Economy*, Vol. 56, February, 1948, pp. 23–34; "The Decisions of a Committee Using a Special Majority," *Econometrica*, Vol. 16, July, 1948, pp. 245–261; "The Elasticity of Committee Decisions with an Altering Size of Majority," *ibid.*, pp. 262–270; and "Un approccio alla teoria delle decisioni di comitato," *Giornale degli economisti e annali di economica*, Vol. 7, Nuova Serie, 1948, pp. 262–284. For the analogy between voting and the market, see especially "The Elasticity of Committee Decisions . . . ," pp. 262, 270; and "Un approccio . . . ," pp. 262–269.

sideration is given to the enjoyment of the decision process as a form of play. There is no need to stress the obvious importance of the desire to play and win the game as such in both economic behavior and political.[18] That such considerations are real and should be considered in determining the mechanics of social choice is not to be doubted; but this is beyond the scope of the present study.

The other meaning of the term "game" is that which has been brought to the attention of economists by Professors von Neumann and Morgenstern.[19] The point here, broadly speaking, is that, once a machinery for making social choices from individual tastes is established, individuals will find it profitable, from a rational point of view, to misrepresent their tastes by their actions, either because such misrepresentation is somehow directly profitable[20] or, more usually, because some other individual will be made so much better off by the first individual's misrepresentation that he could compensate the first individual in such a way that both are better off than if everyone really acted in direct accordance with his tastes. Thus, in an electoral system based on plurality voting, it is notorious that an individual who really favors a minor party candidate will frequently vote for the less undesirable of the major party candidates rather than "throw away his vote." Even in a case where it is possible to construct a procedure showing how to aggregate individual tastes into a consistent social preference pattern, there still remains the problem of devising rules of the game so that individuals will actually express their true tastes even when they are acting rationally. This problem is allied to the problem of constructing games of fair division, in which the rules are to be such that each individual, by playing rationally, will succeed in getting a preassigned fair share; in the case of two people and equal division, the game is the very familiar one in which one player divides the total stock of goods into two parts, and the second player chooses which part he likes.[21]

In addition to ignoring game aspects of the problem of social choice, we will also assume in the present study that individual values are taken as data and are not capable of being altered by the nature of the decision process itself. This, of course, is the standard view in economic theory

[18] Knight has constantly emphasized the importance of play motives in human life; see, for example, the reference in fn. 16. The importance of emulative motives has nowhere been so forcefully stressed as by T. Veblen (*The Theory of the Leisure Class*, New York: The Macmillan Co., 1899).

[19] J. von Neumann and O. Morgenstern, *Theory of Games and Economic Behavior*, second edition, Princeton: Princeton University Press, 1947.

[20] A similar point is made by Bowen, *op. cit.*, pp. 45, 48.

[21] See H. Steinhaus, "The Problem of Fair Division" (abstract), *Econometrica*, Vol. 16, January, 1948, pp. 101–104.

(though the unreality of this assumption has been asserted by such writers as Veblen, Professor J. M. Clark, and Knight [22]) and also in the classical liberal creed.[23] If individual values can themselves be affected by the method of social choice, it becomes much more difficult to learn what is meant by one method's being preferable to another.

Finally, it is assumed that all individuals in the society are rational. The precise meaning of this assumption will be enlarged on in the next chapter.

[22] T. Veblen, *The Theory of the Leisure Class, op. cit.*, and "Why Is Economics Not an Evolutionary Science?" in *The Place of Science in Modern Civilisation and Other Essays*, New York: B. W. Huebsch, 1919, pp. 73–74; J. M. Clark, "Economics and Modern Psychology," in *Preface to Social Economics*, New York: Farrar and Rinehart, 1936, pp. 92–160, and "Realism and Relevance in the Theory of Demand," *Journal of Political Economy*, Vol. 54, August, 1946, pp. 347–351; F. H. Knight, "Ethics and the Economic Interpretation," in *The Ethics of Competition and Other Essays, op. cit.*, pp. 19–40, *passim*.

[23] *"Liberalism takes the individual as given*, and views the social problem as one of right relations between given individuals." (Italics in the original.) F. H. Knight, "Ethics and Economic Reform," in *Freedom and Reform, op. cit.*, p. 69.

CHAPTER II

THE NATURE OF PREFERENCE AND CHOICE

1. MEASURABILITY AND INTERPERSONAL COMPARABILITY OF UTILITY

The viewpoint will be taken here that interpersonal comparison of utilities has no meaning and, in fact, that there is no meaning relevant to welfare comparisons in the measurability of individual utility. The controversy is well-known and hardly need be recited here. During the entire controversy, the proponents of measurable utility have been unable to produce any proposition of economic behavior which could be explained by their hypothesis and not by those of the indifference-curve theorists.[1] Indeed, the only meaning the concepts of utility can be said to have is their indications of actual behavior, and, if any course of behavior can be explained by a given utility function, it has been amply demonstrated that such a course of behavior can be equally well explained by any other utility function which is a strictly increasing function of the first. If we cannot have measurable utility, in this sense, we cannot have interpersonal comparability of utilities a fortiori.

Recently, the issue of measurable utility has been reopened by the results of Professors von Neumann and Morgenstern.[2] These results have been widely misunderstood. They consider a preference pattern not only among certain alternatives but also among alternative probability distributions. Making certain plausible assumptions as to the relations among preferences for related probability distributions, they

[1] Classical demand theory leaves ambiguous the relation between the indifference map of a household and the indifference maps of the individual members thereof. It is the former which is relevant for the behavior of the market. The passage from individual to household maps is a special case of the passage from individual to social orderings; if the present thesis is accepted, household indifference maps can, indeed, only arise from the presence of common standards of value of some sort. But these are, as will be seen, empirically determinable by examination of the individual indifference maps and are not based on some type of intrinsic comparison of intensities of feeling. In what follows we shall ignore the distinction between individual and household indifference maps; this action may be regarded as meaning either that the intra-household aggregation is somehow solved or that that problem is being considered simultaneously with the general problem.

[2] *Op. cit.*, pp. 15–31, 617–632. See also W. S. Vickrey, "Measuring Marginal Utility by Reactions to Risk," *Econometrica*, Vol. 13, October, 1945, pp. 319–333.

find that there is a utility indicator (unique up to a linear transformation) which has the property that the value of the utility function for any probability distribution of certain alternatives is the mathematical expectation of the utility. Put otherwise, there is one way (unique up to a linear transformation) of assigning utilities to probability distributions such that behavior is described by saying that the individual seeks to maximize his expected utility.

This theorem does not, as far as I can see, give any special ethical significance to the particular utility scale found. For instead of using the utility scale found by von Neumann and Morgenstern, we could use the square of that scale; then behavior is described by saying that the individual seeks to maximize the expected value of the square root of his utility. This is not to deny the usefulness of the von Neumann-Morgenstern theorem; what it does say is that among the many different ways of assigning a utility indicator to the preferences among alternative probability distributions, there is one method (more precisely, a whole set of methods which are linear transforms of each other) which has the property of stating the laws of rational behavior in a particularly convenient way. This is a very useful matter from the point of view of developing the descriptive economic theory of behavior in the presence of random events, but it has nothing to do with welfare considerations, particularly if we are interested primarily in making a social choice among alternative policies in which no random elements enter. To say otherwise would be to assert that the distribution of the social income is to be governed by the tastes of individuals for gambling.

The problem of measuring utility has frequently been compared with the problem of measuring temperature. This comparison is very apt. Operationally, the temperature of a body is the volume of a unit mass of a perfect gas placed in contact with it (provided the mass of the gas is small compared with the mass of the body). Why, it might be asked, was not the logarithm of the volume or perhaps the cube root of the volume of the gas used instead? The reason is simply that the general gas equation assumes a particularly simple form when temperature is defined in the way indicated. But there is no deeper significance. Does it make any sense to say that an increase of temperature from 0° to 1° is just as intense as an increase of temperature from 100° to 101°? No more can it be said that there is any meaning in comparing marginal utilities at different levels of well-being.

Even if, for some reason, we should admit the measurability of utility for an individual, there still remains the question of aggregating the individual utilities. At best, it is contended that, for an individual, his utility function is uniquely determined up to a linear transformation;

we must still choose one out of the infinite family of indicators to represent the individual, and the values of the aggregate (say a sum) are dependent on how the choice is made for each individual. In general, there seems to be no method intrinsic to utility measurement which will make the choices compatible.[3] It requires a definite value judgment not derivable from individual sensations to make the utilities of different individuals dimensionally compatible and still a further value judgment to aggregate them according to any particular mathematical formula. If we look away from the mathematical aspects of the matter, it seems to make no sense to add the utility of one individual, a psychic magnitude in his mind, with the utility of another individual. Even Bentham had his doubts on this point.[4]

We will therefore assume throughout this book that the behavior of an individual in making choices is describable by means of a preference scale without any cardinal significance, either individual or interpersonal.

2. A NOTATION FOR PREFERENCES AND CHOICE

In this study it is found convenient to represent preference by a notation not customarily employed in economics, though familiar in mathematics and particularly in symbolic logic. We assume that there is a basic set of alternatives which could conceivably be presented to the chooser. In the theory of consumer's choice, each alternative would be a commodity bundle; in the theory of the firm, each alternative would be a complete decision on all inputs and outputs; in welfare economics, each alternative would be a distribution of commodities and labor re-

[3] It must be granted, though, that, if it is assumed to begin with that all preference scales for individuals are the same (all individuals have the same tastes), then we could choose the utility function the same for all. However, if we take seriously the idea of interpersonal comparison of utilities, we must allow for the possibility that, of two individuals with the same indifference map, one is twice as sensitive as the other, and so the proper utility function for one should be just double that for another. It would be interesting, indeed, to see an operational significance attached to this concept of differing sensitivity.

Von Neumann and Morgenstern (*op. cit.*, pp. 608–616) have considered a case where two individuals have differing powers of discernment, but they have not represented this case by assuming different utilities for the same bundle of goods. Instead, they assume both utility scales can take on only discrete values, though one can take on more such values than the other.

[4] "'Tis in vain to talk of adding quantities which after the addition will continue distinct as they were before, one man's happiness will never be another man's happiness: a gain to one man is no gain to another: you might as well pretend to add 20 apples to 20 pears. . . ." (Quoted by W. C. Mitchell in "Bentham's Felicific Calculus," in *The Backward Art of Spending Money and Other Essays*, New York: McGraw-Hill Book Co., 1937, p. 184.)

quirements. In general, an alternative is a vector; however, in the theory of elections, the alternatives are candidates. These alternatives are mutually exclusive; they are denoted by the small letters x, y, z, $\cdots$. On any given occasion, the chooser has available to him a subset S of all possible alternatives, and he is required to choose one out of this set. The set S is a generalization of the well-known opportunity curve; thus, in the theory of consumer's choice under perfect competition it would be the budget plane. It is assumed further that the choice is made in this way: Before knowing the set S, the chooser considers in turn all possible pairs of alternatives, say x and y, and for each such pair he makes one and only one of three decisions: x is preferred to y, x is indifferent to y, or y is preferred to x. The decisions made for different pairs are assumed to be consistent with each other, so, for example, if x is preferred to y and y to z, then x is preferred to z; similarly, if x is indifferent to y and y to z, then x is indifferent to z. Having this ordering of all possible alternatives, the chooser is now confronted with a particular opportunity set S. If there is one alternative in S which is preferred to all others in S, the chooser selects that one alternative. Suppose, however, there is a subset of alternatives in S such that the alternatives in the subset are each preferred to every alternative not in the subset, while the alternatives in the subset are indifferent to each other. This case would be one in which the highest indifference curve that has a point in common with a given opportunity curve has at least two points in common with it. In this case, the best thing to say is that the choice made in S is the whole-subset; the first case discussed is one in which the subset in question, the choice, contains a single element.

Since we have not restricted the type of sets allowed, a third possibility presents itself; there may be no alternative in S which is preferred or indifferent to all others. That is, for every alternative in S, there is another which is preferred to it. For example, suppose that an individual prefers more money to less and that the alternatives in S include every integral number of dollars. Or, if we wish to require that S is in some sense bounded, consider the sequence of alternatives $\frac{1}{2}$, $\frac{2}{3}$, $\frac{3}{4}$, $\cdots$, $1 - (1/n)$, $\cdots$ dollars. There cannot really be said to be any rational choice in this case. However, this mathematical point will not play any part in the present work.

Preference and indifference are relations between alternatives. Instead of working with two relations, it will be slightly more convenient to use a single relation, "preferred or indifferent." The statement "x is preferred or indifferent to y" will be symbolized by $x R y$. The letter R, by itself, will be the name of the relation and will stand for a knowledge of all pairs such that $x R y$. From our previous discussion, we have that, for any pair of alternatives x and y, either x is preferred to y or y to x, or the two are indifferent. That is, we have assumed that any two alternatives are comparable.[5] But this assumption may be written symbolically, as

AXIOM I: *For all x and y, either $x R y$ or $y R x$.*

A relation R which satisfies Axiom I will be said to be connected. Note that Axiom I is presumed to hold when $x = y$, as well as when x is distinct from y, for we ordinarily say that x is indifferent to itself for any x, and this implies $x R x$.[6] Note also that the word "or" in the statement of Axiom I does not exclude the possibility of both $x R y$ and $y R x$. That word merely asserts that at least one of the two events must occur; both may.

The property mentioned above of consistency in the preferences between different pairs of alternatives may be stated more precisely, as follows: If x is preferred or indifferent to y and y is preferred or indifferent to z, then x must be either preferred or indifferent to z. In symbols,

AXIOM II: *For all x, y, and z, $x R y$ and $y R z$ imply $x R z$.*

A relation satisfying Axiom II is said to be transitive.[7] A relation satisfying both Axioms I and II is termed a weak ordering or sometimes simply an ordering. It is clear that a relation having these two properties taken together does create a ranking of the various alternatives. The adjective "weak" refers to the fact that the ordering does not exclude indifference, i.e., Axioms I and II do not exclude the possibility that for some distinct x and y, both $x R y$ and $y R x$. A strong ordering, on

---

[5] The assumption of comparability of all alternatives is the heart of the integrability controversy in the theory of consumer's choice. See V. Pareto, *Manuel d'économie politique*, deuxième édition, Paris: M. Giard, 1927, pp. 546–569. For some of the paradoxical consequences of nonintegrability (which is equivalent to noncomparability of alternatives not infinitesimally close together), see N. Georgescu-Roegen, "The Pure Theory of Consumer's Behavior," *Quarterly Journal of Economics*, Vol. 50, August, 1936, pp. 545–569. Professor Ville has derived the integrability condition, and therewith the comparability of all alternatives, from some plausible hypotheses on the nature of demand functions (J. Ville, "Sur les conditions d'existence d'une ophélimité totale et d'un indice du niveau des prix," *Annales de l'Université de Lyon*, Section A, Vol. 3, No. 9, 1946, pp. 32–39).

[6] Strictly speaking, a relation is said to be connected if Axiom I holds for $x \neq y$. A relation R is said to be reflexive if, for all x, $x R x$. (See A. Tarski, *Introduction to Logic*, New York: Oxford University Press, 1941, pp. 93–94.) Thus a relation satisfying Axiom I is both connected and reflexive. However, for convenience, we will use the slightly inaccurate terminology in the text, that is, we will use the word "connected" for the longer expression "connected and reflexive."

[7] Tarski, *ibid.*, p. 94.

the other hand, is a ranking in which no ties are possible.[8] A weak ordering is a generalization of the concept "greater than or equal to" applied to real numbers; a strong ordering generalizes the concept "greater than" applied to the same realm.[9]

It might be felt that the two axioms in question do not completely characterize the concept of a preference pattern. For example, we ordinarily feel that not only the relation R but also the relations of (strict) preference and of indifference are transitive. We shall show that, by defining preference and indifference suitably in terms of R, it will follow that all the usually desired properties of preference patterns obtain.

DEFINITION 1: $x P y$ is defined to mean not $y R x$.

The statement "$x P y$" is read "x is preferred to y."

DEFINITION 2: $x I y$ means $x R y$ and $y R x$.

The statement "$x I y$" is read "x is indifferent to y." It is clear that P and I, so defined, correspond to the ordinary notions of preference and indifference, respectively.

LEMMA 1: (a) *For all x, $x R x$.*
　　　　　(b) *If $x P y$, then $x R y$.*
　　　　　(c) *If $x P y$ and $y P z$, then $x P z$.*
　　　　　(d) *If $x I y$ and $y I z$, then $x I z$.*
　　　　　(e) *For all x and y, either $x R y$ or $y P x$.*
　　　　　(f) *If $x P y$ and $y R z$, then $x P z$.*

All these statements are intuitively self-evident from the interpretations placed on the symbols. However, it may be as well to give sketches of the proofs, both to show that Axioms I and II really imply all that we wish to imply about the nature of orderings of alternatives and to illustrate the type of reasoning to be used subsequently.

PROOF: (a) In Axiom I, let $y = x$; then for all x, either $x R x$ or $x R x$, which is to say, $x R x$.

(b) Directly from Definition 1 and Axiom I.

(c) From $x P y$ and $y P z$, we can, by (b), deduce $x R y$. Suppose $z R x$. Then, from $z R x$ and $x R y$, we could deduce $z R y$ by Axiom II. However, from $y P z$, we have, by Definition 1, not $z R y$. Hence the

---

[8] Frequently, indeed, the term "ordering relation" is reserved for strong orderings (Tarski, *ibid.*, pp. 96–97). However, in the present book the unmodified term "ordering" or "ordering relation" will be reserved for weak orderings.

[9] A formal characterization of strong ordering relations will be given later, in discussing the recent work of Professor Duncan Black on the theory of elections; see Chapter VII, Section 2.

supposition $z\,R\,x$ leads to a contradiction, so that we may assert not $z\,R\,x$, or $x\,P\,z$, by Definition 1.

(d) From $x\,I\,y$ and $y\,I\,z$, we can, by Definition 2, deduce $x\,R\,y$ and $y\,R\,z$. From Axiom II, then, $x\,R\,z$. Also from $x\,I\,y$ and $y\,I\,z$, by Definition 2, we have $z\,R\,y$ and $y\,R\,x$, which imply $z\,R\,x$, by Axiom II. Since both $x\,R\,z$ and $z\,R\,x$, $x\,I\,z$ by Definition 2.

(e) Directly from Definition 1.

(f) Suppose $z\,R\,x$. From $z\,R\,x$ and $y\,R\,z$ follows $y\,R\,x$, by Axiom II. But, by Definition 1, $x\,P\,y$ implies not $y\,R\,x$. Hence the supposition $z\,R\,x$ leads to a contradiction. Therefore, not $z\,R\,x$, or $x\,P\,z$.

For clarity, we will avoid the use of the terms "preference scale" or "preference pattern" when referring to R, since we wish to avoid confusion with the concept of preference proper, denoted by P. We will refer to R as an "ordering relation" or "weak ordering relation," or, more simply, as an "ordering" or "weak ordering." The term "preference relation" will refer to the relation P.

In terms of the relation R, we may now define the concept of choice, recalling that in general we must regard the choice from a given set of alternatives as itself a set. If S is the set of alternatives available, which we will term the *environment*,[10] let $C(S)$ be the alternative or alternatives chosen out of S. $C(S)$ is, of course, a subset of S. Each element of $C(S)$ is to be preferred to all elements of S not in $C(S)$ and indifferent to all elements of $C(S)$; and, therefore, if x belongs to $C(S)$, $x\,R\,y$ for all y in S. On the other hand, if in fact $x\,R\,y$ for all y in S and if x belongs to S, then, by Definition 1, there is no element z in S such that $z\,P\,x$. Hence, we may define $C(S)$ formally as follows:

DEFINITION 3: $C(S)$ *is the set of all alternatives x in S such that, for every y in S, $x\,R\,y$.*

$C(S)$, it is to be noted, describes a functional relationship in that it assigns a choice to each possible environment. We may call it the choice function; it is a straightforward generalization of the demand function as it appears in the theory of consumer's choice under perfect competition, the sets S there being budget planes.

Let $[x, y]$ be the set composed of the two alternatives x and y. Suppose $x\,P\,y$. Then $x\,R\,y$, by Lemma 1(b), and $x\,R\,x$, by Lemma 1(a), so that x belongs to $C([x, y])$; but, again by Definition 1, since $x\,P\,y$, not $y\,R\,x$, so that y does not belong to $C([x, y])$, i.e., $C([x, y])$ contains the single element x.

Conversely, suppose $C([x, y])$ contains the single element x. Since y does not belong to $C([x, y])$, not $y\,R\,x$; by Definition 1, $x\,P\,y$.

[10] This term is J. Marschak's.

LEMMA 2: *A necessary and sufficient condition that $x \, P \, y$ is that x be the sole element of $C([x, y])$.*

In case neither $x \, P \, y$ nor $y \, P \, x$, we have, clearly, $x \, I \, y$, and this is equivalent to saying that $C([x, y])$ contains both x and y. If, then, we know $C([x, y])$ for all two-element sets, we have completely defined the relations P and I and therefore the relation R; but, by Definition 3, knowing the relation R completely determines the choice function $C(S)$ for all sets of alternatives. Hence, one of the consequences of the assumptions of rational choice is that the choice in any environment can be determined by a knowledge of the choices in two-element environments.[11]

The representation of the choice mechanism by ordering relations, as suggested above, has certain advantages for the present analysis over the more conventional representations in terms of indifference maps or utility functions. In regard to indifference maps, there is first the obvious advantage of being able to consider alternatives which are represented by vectors with more than two components. Second, the usefulness of an indifference map usually rests to a large measure on the assumption that the chooser desires more of each component of the alternative to less, all other components remaining the same; this assumption serves to orient the chart.[12] Since the present study is concerned with the choice of a social state, each alternative has many components which may be desirable under certain circumstances and undesirable under others. Third, the use of an indifference map involves assumptions of continuity which are unnecessarily restrictive for the

---

[11] Instead of starting, as here, with a weak ordering relation R satisfying certain axioms and then obtaining a choice function, it is possible to impose certain axioms directly on the choice function. It is not hard, in fact, to construct a set of plausible axioms concerning the choice function from which it is possible to deduce that there exists a weak ordering relation which could have generated the choice function, so that the two approaches are logically equivalent. Starting with the choice function instead of the ordering relation is analogous to the approach of Cournot, who started with demand functions having postulated properties instead of deriving those properties from a consideration of indifference maps or utility functions. (A. Cournot, *Mathematical Principles of the Theory of Wealth*, English translation, New York: The Macmillan Co., 1897, pp. 49–50.) The assumptions made by Cournot about the demand function were not very restrictive. More sophisticated treatment of demand from this point of view is to be found in the work of Ville, *op. cit.*, and Samuelson, *op. cit.*, pp. 111–117. Both treatments concern only the case of consumer's choice under perfectly competitive conditions, but suitable generalization to imperfectly competitive environments does not seem impossible.

[12] This brief statement is not accurate when the existence of a point of saturation is assumed. However, the chart is then at least oriented uniformly within each of several large segments, and the interesting economic problems presumably occur in the region where the assumption made in the text holds.

present purpose, especially since, in order to handle such problems as indivisibilities, which have been productive of so much controversy in the field of welfare economics, it is necessary to assume that some of the components of the social state are discrete variables.

As for utility functions, there is first of all the formal difficulty that, if insufficient continuity assumptions are made about the ordering, there may exist no way of assigning real numbers to the various alternatives in such a way as to satisfy the usual requirements of a utility function. In any case, we would simply be replacing the expression $x \, R \, y$ by the expression $U(x) \geq U(y)$, and the structure of all proofs would be unchanged, while the elegance of the whole exposition would be marred by the introduction of the superfluous function $U(x)$, whose significance lies entirely in its ordinal properties. If we are concerned with ordinal properties, it seems better to represent these directly.[13]

3. The Ordering of Social States

In the present study the objects of choice are social states. The most precise definition of a social state would be a complete description of the amount of each type of commodity in the hands of each individual, the amount of labor to be supplied by each individual, the amount of each productive resource invested in each type of productive activity, and the amounts of various types of collective activity, such as municipal services, diplomacy and its continuation by other means, and the erection of statues to famous men. It is assumed that each individual in the community has a definite ordering of all conceivable social states, in terms of their desirability to him. It is not assumed here that an individual's attitude toward different social states is determined exclusively by the commodity bundles which accrue to his lot under each. It is simply assumed that the individual orders all social states by whatever standards he deems relevant. A member of Veblen's leisure class might order the states solely on the criterion of his relative income standing in each; a believer in the equality of man might order them in accordance with some measure of income equality. Indeed, since, as mentioned above, some of the components of the social state, considered as a vector, are collective activities, purely individualistic assumptions are useless in analyzing such problems as the division of the national income between

---

[13] Similarly, in the field of production economics, it seems more natural to express the transformation restrictions by saying that the input-output vector lies in a certain point set than to introduce a transformation function and then subject the operations of the firm to the condition $T = 0$. In this case, the irrelevance of the functional representation is even clearer since, if $F(t) = 0$ if and only if $t = 0$, then $F(T)$ can be used as the transformation function just as well as T.

public and private expenditure. The present notation permits perfect generality in this respect. Needless to say, this generality is not without its price. More information would be available for analysis if the generality were restricted by a prior knowledge of the nature of individual orderings of social states. This problem will be touched on again.

In general, there will, then, be a difference between the ordering of social states according to the direct consumption of the individual and the ordering when the individual adds his general standards of equity (or perhaps his standards of pecuniary emulation).[14] We may refer to the former ordering as reflecting the *tastes* of the individual and the latter as reflecting his *values*. The distinction between the two is by no means clear-cut. An individual with esthetic feelings certainly derives pleasure from his neighbor's having a well-tended lawn. Under the system of a free market, such feelings play no direct part in social choice; yet psychologically they differ only slightly from the pleasure in one's own lawn. Intuitively, of course, we feel that not all the possible preferences which an individual might have ought to count; his preferences for matters which are "none of his business" should be irrelevant. Without challenging this view, I should like to emphasize that the decision as to which preferences are relevant and which are not is itself a value judgment and cannot be settled on an a priori basis. From a formal point of view, one cannot distinguish between an individual's dislike for having his grounds ruined by factory smoke and his extreme distaste for the existence of heathenism in Central Africa. There are probably not a few individuals in this country who would regard the former feeling as irrelevant for social policy and the latter as relevant, though the majority would probably reverse the judgment. I merely wish to emphasize here that we must look at the entire system of values, including values about values, in seeking for a truly general theory of social welfare.

It is the ordering according to values which takes into account all the desires of the individual, including the highly important socializing desires, and which is primarily relevant for the achievement of a social maximum. The market mechanism, however, takes into account only the ordering according to tastes. This distinction is the analogue, on the side of consumption, of the divergence between social and private costs in production developed by Professor Pigou.[15]

[14] This distinction has been stressed to the author by M. Friedman, The University of Chicago.

[15] A. C. Pigou, *The Economics of Welfare*, London: Macmillan and Co., 1920, Part II, Chapter VI. For the analogy, see Samuelson, *op. cit.*, p. 224; Reder, *op. cit.*, pp. 64–67; G. Tintner, "A Note on Welfare Economics," *Econometrica*, Vol. 14, January, 1946, pp. 69–78.

As for notation, we will let R_i be the ordering relation for alternative social states from the standpoint of individual i. Sometimes, when several different ordering relations are being considered for the same individual, the symbols will be distinguished by adding a superscript. Corresponding to the ordering relation R_i, we have the (strict) preference relation P_i and the indifference relation I_i. If the symbol for the ordering has a prime or second attached (thus, R_i', R_i''), then the corresponding symbols for preference and indifference will have the prime or second attached, respectively.

Similarly, society as a whole will be considered provisionally to have a social ordering relation for alternative social states, which will be designated by R, sometimes with a prime or second. Social preference and indifference will be denoted by P and I, respectively, primes or seconds being attached when they are attached to the relation R.

Throughout this analysis it will be assumed that individuals are rational, by which is meant that the ordering relations R_i satisfy Axioms I and II. The problem will be to construct an ordering relation for society as a whole that will also reflect rational choice-making so that R may also be assumed to satisfy Axioms I and II.

4. A DIGRESSION ON RATIONALITY AND CHOICE

The concept of rationality used throughout this study is at the heart of modern economic analysis, and it cannot be denied that it has great intuitive appeal; but closer analysis reveals difficulties. These may be illustrated by consideration of the modern developments in the theory of games and, in particular, the theory of zero-sum two-person games.[16]

[16] The theory of games involving more than two persons or games in which the sum of the payments to the various players is not independent of the methods of play is still in a dubious state despite the mathematically beautiful development in von Neumann and Morgenstern, *op. cit.*, Chapters V–XII. For example, the highly developed mechanism of compensations needed for their theory of rational behavior in such games appears to have little counterpart in the real world, as was pointed out by Professor Bain in another connection (J. S. Bain, "Output Quotas in Imperfect Cartels," *Quarterly Journal of Economics*, Vol. 62, August, 1948, pp. 617–622). On the other hand, there can be little doubt that the theory of rational play of a zero-sum two-person game has been completely solved, at least under certain restrictive assumptions as to the risk-neutrality of the players and as to the completeness of their information concerning the rules of the game. (See J. von Neumann, "Zur Theorie der Gesellschaftsspiele," *Mathematische Annalen*, Vol. 100, August, 1928, pp. 295–320; von Neumann and Morgenstern, *op. cit.*, Chapters III–IV.) Hence the theory of behavior in zero-sum two-person games affords some sort of check on the concepts of rationality derived to a large extent by analogy with the static theory of the firm under perfect competition.

As noted in Chapter II, Section 2, one of the consequences of the assumption of rationality is that the choice to be made from any set of alternatives can be determined by the choices made between pairs of alternatives. Suppose, however, that the situation is such that the chooser is never confronted with choices between pairs of alternatives; instead, the environment may always involve many alternatives. Indeed, that is precisely the situation in the theory of consumer's choice under perfect competition; the actual environment is always a whole line or plane. But, under certain plausible conditions, we can say that the choices made from the actual environments can be explained as though they were derived from choices between pairs of alternatives; and, at least conceptually, it makes sense to imagine the choices actually being made from pairs of alternatives.

Superficially, the theory of rational behavior in the zero-sum two-person game seems to fall into the same pattern. We could imagine each of the players considering all his possible strategies in turn, ordering them on the basis of the minimum profit (or maximum loss) that he could expect under each, and then choosing his best strategy by going as high up on the resulting scale as he can. But the only reason why we regard this solution as truly rational is that, if both players follow it, neither one will have any incentive to change his strategy even if he finds out the opponent's. This is the essence of the famous min-max or saddle-point theorem. The validity of this theorem, however, arises from the fact that every time we admit a set of pure strategies into the player's environment, we also admit all mixtures of them, i.e., all probability distributions over such a set of pure strategies. Hence, the environment (set of admissible strategies), if it contains more than one strategy, automatically contains an infinite number. Nor can we even conceptually imagine the choice between two strategies; for, if this limitation were real, a saddle-point would exist only in special cases, and the ordering of the strategies by minimum profit would not lead to a solution having the stability properties described above.

Thus, the model of rational choice as built up from pair-wise comparisons does not seem to suit well the case of rational behavior in the described game situation. It seems that the essential point is, and this is of general bearing, that, if conceptually we imagine a choice being made between two alternatives, we cannot exclude any probability distribution over those two choices as a possible alternative. The precise shape of a formulation of rationality which takes the last point into account or the consequences of such a reformulation on the theory of choice in general or the theory of social choice in particular cannot be foreseen; but it is at least a possibility, to which attention should be drawn, that the paradox to be discussed below might be resolved by such a broader concept of rationality.

Many writers have felt that the assumption of rationality, in the sense of a one-dimensional ordering of all possible alternatives, is absolutely necessary for economic theorizing; for example, Professor Rothschild remarks, "Unless economic units act in conformity with some rational pattern no general theory about what would follow from certain premises would be possible." [17]   There seems to be no logical necessity for this viewpoint; we could just as well build up our economic theory on other assumptions as to the structure of choice functions if the facts seemed to call for it.[18]   The work of the institutionalist school may be regarded in part as such an attempt, though no systematic treatment has emerged.

The concept of choice functions not built up from orderings seems to correspond to Rothschild's "real irrationality"; however, such choice functions need not be the product of impulsive behavior but may conceivably arise from full reflection, as in the theory of games discussed above.

[17] K. W. Rothschild, "The Meaning of Rationality: A Note on Professor Lange's Article," *Review of Economic Studies*, Vol. 14, No. 1, 1946–47, p. 50. Rothschild also attributes this view to Professor Lange, but there seems to be a misinterpretation. Lange regards the assumption of rationality (which he identifies with ordering) as a highly convenient postulate, if true, but not necessary. (O. Lange, "The Scope and Method of Economics," *ibid.*, Vol. 13, No. 1, 1945–46, p. 30.)

[18] Like Lange, the present author regards economics as an attempt to discover uniformities in a certain part of reality and not as the drawing of logical consequences from a certain set of assumptions regardless of their relevance to actuality. Simplified theory-building is an absolute necessity for empirical analysis; but it is a means, not an end.

Chapter III

THE SOCIAL WELFARE FUNCTION

1. Formal Statement of the Problem of Social Choice

I will largely restate Professor Bergson's formulation of the problem of making welfare judgments [1] in the terminology here adopted. The various arguments of his social welfare function are the components of what I have here termed the social state, so that essentially he is describing the process of assigning a numerical social utility to each social state, the aim of society then being described by saying that it seeks to maximize the social utility or social welfare subject to whatever technological or resource constraints are relevant or, put otherwise, that it chooses the social state yielding the highest possible social welfare within the environment. As with any type of behavior described by maximization, the measurability of social welfare need not be assumed; all that matters is the existence of a social ordering satisfying Axioms I and II. As before, all that is needed to define such an ordering is to know the relative ranking of each pair of alternatives.

The relative ranking of a fixed pair of alternative social states will vary, in general, with changes in the values of at least some individuals; to assume that the ranking does not change with any changes in individual values is to assume, with traditional social philosophy of the Platonic realist variety, that there exists an objective social good defined independently of individual desires. This social good, it was frequently held, could best be apprehended by the methods of philosophic inquiry. Such a philosophy could be and was used to justify government by the elite, secular or religious, although we shall see below that the connection is not a necessary one.

To the nominalist temperament of the modern period, the assumption of the existence of the social ideal in some Platonic realm of being was meaningless. The utilitarian philosophy of Jeremy Bentham and his followers sought instead to ground the social good on the good of individuals. The hedonist psychology associated with utilitarian philosophy was further used to imply that each individual's good was identical with his desires. Hence, the social good was in some sense to be a

---

[1] Bergson, "A Reformulation . . . ," *op. cit., passim.*

composite of the desires of individuals. A viewpoint of this type serves as a justification of both political democracy and laissez-faire economics or at least an economic system involving free choice of goods by consumers and of occupations by workers.

The hedonist psychology finds its expression here in the assumption that individuals' behavior is expressed by individual ordering relations R_i. Utilitarian philosophy is expressed by saying that for each pair of social states the choice depends on the ordering relations of all individuals, i.e., depends on $R_1, \cdots, R_n$, where n is the number of individuals in the community. Put otherwise, the whole social ordering relation R is to be determined by the individual ordering relations for social states, $R_1, \cdots, R_n$. We do not exclude here the possibility that some or all of the choices between pairs of social states made by society might be independent of the preferences of certain particular individuals, just as a function of several variables might be independent of some of them.

DEFINITION 4: *By a* social welfare function *will be meant a process or rule which, for each set of individual orderings $R_1, \cdots, R_n$ for alternative social states (one ordering for each individual), states a corresponding social ordering of alternative social states, R.*

As a matter of notation, we will let R be the social ordering corresponding to the set of individual orderings $R_1, \cdots, R_n$, the correspondence being that established by a given social welfare function; if primes or seconds are added to the symbols for the individual orderings, primes or seconds will be added to the symbol for the corresponding social ordering.

There is some difference between the concept of social welfare function used here and that employed by Bergson. The individual orderings which enter as arguments into the social welfare function as defined here refer to the values of individuals rather than to their tastes. Bergson supposes individual values to be such as to yield a social value judgment leading to a particular rule for determining the allocation of productive resources and the distribution of leisure and final products in accordance with individual tastes. In effect, the social welfare function described here is a method of choosing which social welfare function of the Bergson type will be applicable, though, of course, I do not exclude the possibility that the social choice actually arrived at will not be consistent with the particular value judgments formulated by Bergson. But in the formal aspect the difference between the two definitions of social welfare function is not too important. In Bergson's treatment, the tastes of individuals (each for his own consumption) are represented by utility functions, i.e., essentially by ordering relations; hence the Bergson social welfare function is also a rule for assigning to each set of individual orderings a social ordering of social states. Furthermore, as already indicated, no sharp line can be drawn between tastes and values.

A special type of social welfare function would be one which assigns the same social ordering for every set of individual orderings. In this case, of course, social choices are completely independent of individual tastes, and we are back in the Platonic case.

If we do not wish to require any prior knowledge of the tastes of individuals before specifying our social welfare function, that function will have to be defined for every logically possible set of individual orderings. Such a social welfare function would be universal in the sense that it would be applicable to any community. This ideal seems to be implicit in Benthamite social ethics and in its latter-day descendant, welfare economics.

However, we need not ask ourselves if such a universal social welfare function can be defined. Let an *admissible* set of individual ordering relations be a set for which the social welfare function defines a corresponding social ordering, i.e., a relation satisfying Axioms I and II. A universal social welfare function would be one for which every set of individual orderings was admissible. However, we may feel on some sort of a priori grounds that certain types of individual orderings need not be admissible. For example, it has frequently been assumed or implied in welfare economics that each individual values different social states solely according to his consumption under them. If this be the case, we should only require that our social welfare function be defined for those sets of individual orderings which are of the type described; only such should be admissible.

We will, however, suppose that our a priori knowledge about the occurrence of individual orderings is incomplete, to the extent that there are at least three among all the alternatives under consideration for which the ordering by any given individual is completely unknown in advance. That is, every logically possible set of individual orderings of a certain set S of three alternatives can be obtained from some admissible set of individual orderings of all alternatives. More formally, we have

CONDITION 1: *Among all the alternatives there is a set S of three alternatives such that, for any set of individual orderings $T_1, \cdots, T_n$ of the alternatives in S, there is an admissible set of individual orderings $R_1, \cdots, R_n$ of all the alternatives such that, for each individual i, $x R_i y$ if and only if $x T_i y$ for x and y in S.*

Condition 1, it should be emphasized, is a restriction on the form of the social welfare function since, by definition of an admissible set of individual orderings, we are requiring that, for some sufficiently wide range of sets of individual orderings, the social welfare function give rise to a true social ordering.

We also wish to impose several other apparently reasonable conditions on the social welfare function.

2. Positive Association of Social and Individual Values

Since we are trying to describe social welfare and not some sort of illfare, we must assume that the social welfare function is such that the social ordering responds positively to alterations in individual values, or at least not negatively. Hence, if one alternative social state rises or remains still in the ordering of every individual without any other change in those orderings, we expect that it rises, or at least does not fall, in the social ordering.

This condition can be reformulated as follows: Suppose, in the initial position, that individual values are given by a set of individual orderings $R_1, \cdots, R_n$, and suppose that the corresponding social ordering R is such that $x \, P \, y$, where x and y are two given alternatives and P is the preference relation corresponding to R, i.e., defined in terms of R in accordance with Definition 1. Suppose values subsequently change in such a way that for each individual the only change in relative rankings, if any, is that x is higher in the scale than before. If we call the new individual orderings (those expressing the new set of values) $R_1{}', \cdots, R_n{}'$ and the social ordering corresponding to them R', then we would certainly expect that $x \, P' \, y$, where P' is the preference relation corresponding to R'. This is a natural requirement since no individual ranks x lower than he formerly did; if society formerly ranked x above y, we should certainly expect that it still does.

We have still to express formally the condition that x be not lower on each individual's scale while all other comparisons remain unchanged. The last part of the condition can be expressed by saying that, among pairs of alternatives neither of which is x, the relation $R_i{}'$ will obtain for those pairs for which the relation R_i holds and only such; in symbols, for all $x' \neq x$ and $y' \neq x$, $x' \, R_i{}' \, y'$ if and only if $x' \, R_i \, y'$. The condition that x be not lower on the $R_i{}'$ scale than x was on the R_i scale means that x is preferred on the $R_i{}'$ scale to any alternative to which it was preferred on the old (R_i) scale and also that x is preferred or indifferent to any alternative to which it was formerly indifferent. The two conditions of the last sentence, taken together, are equivalent to the following two conditions: (1) x is preferred on the new scale to any alternative to which it was formerly preferred; (2) x is preferred or indifferent on the new scale to any alternative to which it was formerly preferred or indifferent.   In symbols, for all y', $x\ R_i\ y'$ implies $x\ R_i'\ y'$, and $x\ P_i\ y'$ implies $x\ P_i'\ y'$.   We can now state the second condition which our social welfare function must satisfy.

CONDITION 2: *Let* R_1, $\cdots$, R_n *and* R_1', $\cdots$, R_n' *be two sets of individual ordering relations, R and R' the corresponding social orderings, and P and P' the corresponding social preference relations.   Suppose that for each i the two individual ordering relations are connected in the following ways: for x' and y' distinct from a given alternative x, $x'\ R_i'\ y'$ if and only if $x'\ R_i\ y'$; for all y', $x\ R_i\ y'$ implies $x\ R_i'\ y'$; for all y', $x\ P_i\ y'$ implies $x\ P_i'\ y'$.   Then, if $x\ P\ y$, $x\ P'\ y$.*

3. THE INDEPENDENCE OF IRRELEVANT ALTERNATIVES

If we consider $C(S)$, the choice function derived from the social ordering R, to be the choice which society would actually make if confronted with a set of alternatives S, then, just as for a single individual, the choice made from any fixed environment S should be independent of the very existence of alternatives outside of S.   For example, suppose that an election system has been devised whereby each individual lists all the candidates in order of his preference and then, by a preassigned procedure, the winning candidate is derived from these lists.   (All actual election procedures are of this type, although in most the entire list is not required for the choice.)   Suppose that an election is held, with a certain number of candidates in the field, each individual filing his list of preferences, and then one of the candidates dies.   Surely the social choice should be made by taking each of the individual's preference lists, blotting out completely the dead candidate's name, and considering only the orderings of the remaining names in going through the procedure of determining the winner.   That is, the choice to be made among the set S of surviving candidates should be independent of the preferences of individuals for candidates not in S.   To assume otherwise would be to make the result of the election dependent on the obviously accidental circumstance of whether a candidate died before or after the date of polling.   Therefore, we may require of our social welfare function that the choice made by society from a given environment depend only on the orderings of individuals among the alternatives in that environment. Alternatively stated, if we consider two sets of individual orderings such that, for each individual, his ordering of those particular alternatives in a given environment is the same each time, then we require that the choice made by society from that environment be the same when individual values are given by the first set of orderings as they are when given by the second.

CONDITION 3: *Let $R_1, \cdots, R_n$ and $R_1', \cdots, R_n'$ be two sets of individual orderings and let $C(S)$ and $C'(S)$ be the corresponding social choice functions. If, for all individuals i and all x and y in a given environment S, $x R_i y$ if and only if $x R_i' y$, then $C(S)$ and $C'(S)$ are the same* (independence of irrelevant alternatives).

The reasonableness of this condition can be seen by consideration of the possible results in a method of choice which does not satisfy Condition 3, the rank-order method of voting frequently used in clubs.[2] With a finite number of candidates, let each individual rank all the candidates, i.e., designate his first-choice candidate, second-choice candidate, etc. Let preassigned weights be given to the first, second, etc., choices, the higher weight to the higher choice, and then let the candidate with the highest weighted sum of votes be elected. In particular, suppose that there are three voters and four candidates, $x, y, z,$ and w. Let the weights for the first, second, third, and fourth choices be 4, 3, 2, and 1, respectively. Suppose that individuals 1 and 2 rank the candidates in the order $x, y, z,$ and w, while individual 3 ranks them in the order $z, w, x,$ and y. Under the given electoral system, x is chosen. Then, certainly, if y is deleted from the ranks of the candidates, the system applied to the remaining candidates should yield the same result, especially since, in this case, y is inferior to x according to the tastes of every individual; but, if y is in fact deleted, the indicated electoral system would yield a tie between x and z.

A similar problem arises in ranking teams in a contest which is essentially individual, e.g., a foot race in which there are several runners from each college, and where it is desired to rank the institutions on the basis of the rankings of the individual runners. This problem has been studied by Professor E. V. Huntington,[3] who showed by means of an example that the usual method of team scoring in those circumstances, a method analogous to the rank-order method of voting, was inconsistent with a condition analogous to Condition 3, which Huntington termed the postulate of relevancy.

The condition of the independence of irrelevant alternatives implies that in a generalized sense all methods of social choice are of the type of

---

[2] This example was suggested by a discussion with G. E. Forsythe, National Bureau of Standards.

[3] E. V. Huntington, "A Paradox in the Scoring of Competing Teams," *Science*, Vol. 88, September 23, 1938, pp. 287–288. I am indebted for this reference to J. Marschak.

voting. If S is the set $[x, y]$ consisting of the two alternatives x and y, Condition 3 tells us that the choice between x and y is determined solely by the preferences of the members of the community as between x and y. That is, if we know which members of the community prefer x to y, which are indifferent, and which prefer y to x, then we know what choice the community makes. Knowing the social choices made in pairwise comparisons in turn determines the entire social ordering and therewith the social choice function $C(S)$ for all possible environments. Condition 2 guarantees that voting for a certain alternative has the usual effect of making surer that that alternative will be adopted.

Condition 1 says, in effect, that, as the environment varies and individual orderings remain fixed, the different choices made shall bear a certain type of consistent relation to each other. Conditions 2 and 3, on the other hand, suppose a fixed environment and say that, for certain particular types of variation in individual values, the various choices made have a certain type of consistency.

4. The Condition of Citizens' Sovereignty

We certainly wish to assume that the individuals in our society are free to choose, by varying their values, among the alternatives available. That is, we do not wish our social welfare function to be such as to prevent us, by its very definition, from expressing a preference for some given alternative over another.

Definition 5: *A social welfare function will be said to be imposed if, for some pair of distinct alternatives x and y, $x R y$ for any set of individual orderings $R_1, \cdots, R_n$, where R is the social ordering corresponding to $R_1, \cdots, R_n$.*

In other words, when the social welfare function is imposed, there is some pair of alternatives x and y such that the community can never express a preference for y over x no matter what the tastes of all individuals are, even if all individuals prefer y to x; some preferences are taboo. (Note that, by Definition 1, asserting that $x R y$ holds for all sets of individual orderings is equivalent to asserting that $y P x$ never holds.)

At the beginning of this study, allusion was made to the type of social choice in which decisions are made in accordance with a customary code. It is arguable whether or not Definition 5 catches the essence of the intuitive idea of conventional choice. In the true case of customary restraints on social choice, presumably the restraints are not felt as such but really are part of the tastes of the individuals. The problems here involve psychological subtleties; can we speak, in the given situation, of true desires of the individual members of the society which are in conflict with the custom of the group?

If the answer to the last question is yes, then Definition 5 is indeed a correct formalization of the concept of conventionality. But we need not give a definite answer, and this is especially fortunate since an examination of the question would take us very far afield indeed. For certainly we wish to impose on our social welfare function the condition that it not be imposed in the sense of Definition 5; we certainly wish all choices to be possible if unanimously desired by the group. If Definition 5 is not a model of customary choice, it is at least a model of external control, such as obtains in a colony or an occupied country.

CONDITION 4: *The social welfare function is not to be imposed.*

Condition 4 is stronger than need be for the present argument. Some decisions as between given pairs of alternatives may be assumed to be imposed. All that is required really is that there be a set S of three alternatives such that the choice between any pair is not constrained in advance by the social welfare function. This set S must also have the properties indicated in Condition 1.

If the answer to the question asked earlier is that there is no sense in speaking of a conflict of wills between the individual and the sacred code, then we have a situation in which it is known in advance that the individual orderings of social alternatives conform to certain restrictions, i.e., that certain of the choices made by individuals are preassigned. In that case, we might desire that the social welfare function be defined only for sets of individual orderings compatible with the known socio-ethical norms of the community; this requirement may involve a weakening of Condition 1. This point will be discussed at greater length in Chapter VII.

It should also be noted that Condition 4 excludes the Platonic case discussed in Section 1 of this chapter. It expresses fully the idea that all social choices are determined by individual desires. In conjunction with Condition 2 (which insures that the determination is in the direction of agreeing with individual desires), Condition 4 expresses the same idea as Bergson's Fundamental Value Propositions of Individual Preference, which state that, between two alternatives between which all individuals but one are indifferent, the community will prefer one over the other or be indifferent between the two according as the one indi-

vidual prefers one over the other or is indifferent between the two.[4]
Conditions 2 and 4 together correspond to the usual concept of consumer's sovereignty; since we are here referring to values rather than
tastes, we might refer to them as expressing the idea of citizens'
sovereignty.

5. THE CONDITION OF NONDICTATORSHIP

A second form of social choice not of a collective character is the
choice by dictatorship. In its pure form, it means that social choices
are to be based solely on the preferences of one man. That is, whenever the dictator prefers x to y, so does society. If the dictator is indifferent between x and y, presumably he will then leave the choice up
to some or all of the other members of society.

DEFINITION 6: *A social welfare function is said to be dictatorial if there
exists an individual i such that, for all x and y, $x \, P_i \, y$ implies $x \, P \, y$ regardless of the orderings $R_1, \cdots, R_n$ of all individuals other than i, where
P is the social preference relation corresponding to $R_1, \cdots, R_n$.*

Since we are interested in the construction of collective methods of
social choice, we wish to exclude dictatorial social welfare functions.

CONDITION 5: *The social welfare function is not to be dictatorial* (nondictatorship).

Again, it cannot be claimed that Definition 6 is a true model of actual
dictatorship. There is normally an element of consent by the members
of the community or at least a good many of them. This may be expressed formally by saying that the desires of those individuals include
a liking for having social decisions made by a dictator [5] or at least a
liking for the particular social decisions which they expect the dictator
to make. The idea of a taste for dictatorship on the part of individuals
will be discussed in Chapter VII at somewhat greater length. However,
in any case, Condition 5 is certainly a reasonable one to impose on the
form of the social welfare function.

We have now imposed five apparently reasonable conditions on the
construction of a social welfare function. These conditions are, of course,

[4] Bergson, "A Reformulation . . . ," *op. cit.*, pp. 318–320. The Fundamental
Value Propositions of Individual Preference are not, strictly speaking, implied by
Conditions 2 and 4 (in conjunction with Conditions 1 and 3), though something
very similar to them is so implied; see Consequence 3 in Chapter V, Section 3. A
slightly stronger form of Condition 2 than that stated here would suffice to yield the
desired implication.

[5] See E. Fromm, *Escape from Freedom*, New York: Rinehart and Co., 1941, 305 pp.

value judgments and could be called into question; taken together they express the doctrines of citizens' sovereignty and rationality in a very general form, with the citizens being allowed to have a wide range of values. The question raised is that of constructing a social ordering of all conceivable alternative social states from any given set of individual orderings of those social states, the method of construction being in accordance with the value judgments of citizens' sovereignty and rationality as expressed in Conditions 1–5.

6. THE SUMMATION OF UTILITIES

It may be instructive to consider that proposed social welfare function which has the longest history, the Bentham-Edgeworth sum of individual utilities. As it stands, this form seems to be excluded by the entire nature of the present approach, since, in Chapter II, Section 1, we agreed to reject the idea of cardinal utility, and especially of interpersonally comparable utility. However, presumably the sum of utilities could be reformulated in a way which depends only on the individual orderings and not on the utility indicators. This seems to be implied by Bergson's discussion of this social welfare function; [6] though he presents a number of cogent arguments against the sum-of-utilities form, he does not find that it contradicts the Fundamental Value Propositions of Individual Preference (see Section 4 above), which he would have to if he did not consider that form to be determined by the individual orderings. The only way that I can see of making the sum of utilities depend only on the indifference loci is the following: Since to each individual ordering there corresponds an infinite number of utility indicators, set up an arbitrary rule which assigns to each indifference map one of its utility indicators; then the sum of the particular utility indicators chosen by the rule is a function of the individual orderings and can be used to establish a social ordering.

Obviously, this formation of the sum of utilities will lead to different decisions in a given situation with different choices of the rule. For any rule, Condition 1 is satisfied. However, Conditions 2 and 3 essentially prescribe that, for a given environment, the choice made shall vary in a particular way with certain variations in the orderings of individuals. This being so, it is clear that for the sum of utilities to satisfy Conditions 2 and 3, it would be necessary for the rule to be stringently limited; in fact, the general theorem, established in Chapter V, guarantees that the only rules which would make the sum of utilities satisfy Conditions 2 and 3, if any, lead it to violate either Condition 4 or Condi-

[6] Bergson, "A Reformulation . . . ," *op. cit.*, pp. 324, 327–328.

tion 5. Indeed, according to Theorem 3 in Chapter VI, Section 3, the same would be true even if it were assumed that the utility of each individual depended solely on his own consumption. I have not been able to construct a special proof of this fact for the sum of utilities which is essentially different from the proof of the general theorem.

It may be of interest, however, to consider a particular rule for assigning utility indicators to individual orderings.[7] Assume that the individual orderings for probability distributions over alternatives obey the axioms of von Neumann and Morgenstern;[8] then there is a method of assigning utilities to the alternatives, unique up to a linear transformation, which has the property that the probability distributions over alternatives are ordered by the expected value of utility. Assume that for each individual there is always one alternative which is preferred or indifferent to all other conceivable alternatives and one to which all other alternatives are preferred or indifferent. Then, for each individual, the utility indicator can be defined uniquely among the previously defined class, which is unique up to a linear transformation, by assigning the utility 1 to the best conceivable alternative and 0 to the worst conceivable alternative. This assignment of values is designed to make individual utilities interpersonally comparable.

It is not hard to see that the suggested assignment of utilities is extremely unsatisfactory. Suppose there are altogether three alternatives and three individuals. Let two of the individuals have the utility 1 for alternative x, .9 for y, and 0 for z; and let the third individual have the utility 1 for y, .5 for x and 0 for z. According to the above criterion, y is preferred to x. Clearly, z is a very undesirable alternative since each individual regards it as worst. If z were blotted out of existence, it should not make any difference to the final outcome; yet, under the proposed rule for assigning utilities to alternatives, doing so would cause the first two individuals to have utility 1 for x and 0 for y, while the third individual has utility 0 for x and 1 for y, so that the ordering by sum of utilities would cause x to be preferred to y.

A simple modification of the above argument shows that the proposed rule does not lead to a sum-of-utilities social welfare function consistent with Condition 3. Instead of blotting z out of existence, let the individual orderings change in such a way that the first two individuals find z indifferent to x and the third now finds z indifferent to y, while the relative positions of x and y are unchanged in all individual orderings. Then the assignment of utilities to x and y becomes the same as it

[7] This particular rule was suggested by A. Kaplan.
[8] See fn. 1, Chapter II.

became in the case of blotting out z entirely, so that again the choice between x and y is altered, contrary to Condition 3.

The above result appears to depend on the particular method of choosing the units of utility. But this is not true, although the paradox is not so obvious in other cases. The point is, in general, that the choice of two particular alternatives to produce given utilities (say 0 and 1) is an arbitrary act, and this arbitrariness is ultimately reflected in the failure of the implied social welfare function to satisfy one of the conditions laid down.

CHAPTER IV

THE COMPENSATION PRINCIPLE

1. THE PAYMENT OF COMPENSATION

To clarify further the difficulties in constructing a social welfare function, let us consider another proposed form, the compensation principle. This term has been used to denote two different, though related, methods of forming social choices from individual orderings.[1] One is the dictum that, if there is a method of paying compensations such that, if society changes from state y to state x and then makes compensations according to the rule, each individual prefers the resultant state to state y (or each individual either prefers the resultant state to state y or is indifferent between them and at least one individual actually prefers the resultant state), then the community ought to prefer x to y *if the compensations are made.*

This formulation is certainly not debatable except perhaps on a philosophy of systematically denying people whatever they want. Actually, it is a rather roundabout way of saying something simple. For what is relevant is not the state x before the compensations are paid but the state which is achieved by first changing from y to x and then making the indicated compensations. It is really the latter state which is preferred to y; let us redesignate this state by x. In the language we have been using, we may say that $x \, P \, y$ if $x \, R_i \, y$ for all i and $x \, P_i \, y$ for at least one value of i, where P is the social preference relation corresponding to the individual orderings $R_1, \cdots, R_n$. If we supplement this with the statement that $x \, I \, y$ if $x \, I_i \, y$ for all i, then we have simply Professor Bergson's Fundamental Value Propositions of Individual Preference.[2]

Let us now define a relation, $x \, Q \, y$, as follows:

(1) $\qquad\qquad x \, Q \, y$ *means that, for all i, $x \, R_i \, y$.*

It has been assumed that, for all i, R_i is a weak ordering relation and so satisfies Axioms I and II. From Lemma 1(u),

(2) $\qquad\qquad\qquad$ *for all i, $x \, R_i \, x$.*

---

[1] See Reder, *op. cit.*, Chapter 1, especially pp. 14, 17.
[2] See fn. 4, Chapter III.

From Axiom II,

(3)   *for all i, $x R_i y$ and $y R_i z$ imply $x R_i z$.*

From (2) and (1), it is clear that,

(4)   *for all x, $x Q x$.*

Suppose that we have $x Q y$ and $y Q z$; then, for each i, $x R_i y$ and $y R_i z$, by (1), so that, for each i, $x R_i z$, by (3). But then, by (1), $x Q z$. Therefore,

(5)   *for all x, y, and z, $x Q y$ and $y Q z$ imply $x Q z$.*

For convenience, we will introduce a formal definition for relations having properties (4) and (5).

DEFINITION 7: *Q is said to be a quasi-ordering if,*
(a) *for all x, $x Q x$;*
(b) *for all x, y, and z, $x Q y$ and $y Q z$ imply $x Q z$.*[3]

Note that under this definition some pairs of alternatives can be compared under a given quasi-ordering while there may be other pairs that are not comparable, i.e., such that neither $x Q y$ nor $y Q x$.

We are saying, then, that the particular relation Q defined by (1) is a quasi-ordering of the space of alternatives. Suppose that, in the case of our particular Q, we know that the individual orderings $R_1, \cdots, R_n$ are such that $x Q y$. Then we certainly feel that we could assert that $x R y$, though we would not be able to assert that $x P y$, since, for example, we can have $x Q y$ because $x I_i y$ for each i.

Suppose, in the case of the relation Q defined by (1), we know that the individual orderings are such that $x Q y$ and not $y Q x$. From (1), this means that for all i, $x R_i y$, while, for at least one i, not $y R_i x$, which, by Lemma 1(e), means that, for at least one i, $x P_i y$. This is the assumption of the form of the compensation principle with which we started. We would feel it reasonable to require that, under these circumstances, $x P y$. Summing up, the relations between Q and the social ordering R are that $x Q y$ implies $x R y$, and that $x Q y$ and not $y Q x$ imply $x R y$ and not $y R x$. We shall introduce this as a general definition.

DEFINITION 8: *R is said to be compatible with Q if*
(a) *R is a weak ordering;*
(b) *Q is a quasi-ordering;*
(c) *for all x and y, $x Q y$ implies $x R y$;*
(d) *for all x and y, $x Q y$ and not $y Q x$ imply not $y R x$.*

[3] G. Birkhoff, *Lattice Theory*, New York: American Mathematical Society, 1940, p. 7.

Let the particular quasi-ordering Q defined by (1) be known as the *unanimity quasi-ordering*. It depends, of course, on the particular set of individual orderings. The "compensation principle" discussed in this section may be restated as follows: For any set of individual orderings, the corresponding social ordering is compatible with the unanimity quasi-ordering. As already noted (fn. 4, Chapter III), this principle is not deducible from Conditions 1–5 as they now stand, but it would be deducible if a slight modification in the statement of Condition 2 were made.

This formulation suggests the following problem: If x and y are both in an environment S, and $x\,Q\,y$ but not $y\,Q\,x$, then $x\,P\,y$, so that, by Definition 3, y would not belong to $C(S)$. Hence, if we could find all alternatives y in S for which there exists an x in S such that $x\,Q\,y$ and not $y\,Q\,x$, we could exclude all such y from consideration in seeking to determine $C(S)$; or, if we could find all alternatives x for which there do not exist any y such that $y\,Q\,x$ but not $x\,Q\,y$, we would know that $C(S)$ must be contained among such alternatives. Alternatives x having this property may be termed maximal.

The study of the last problem, under particular assumptions as to the nature of S and of the individual orderings, has indeed been the main content of what is sometimes called the new welfare economics.[4] Investigation along these lines has been encouraged by the idea that these results are independent of any but the most indisputable value judgments. But though the study of maximal alternatives is possibly

[4] The first formulation of the problem in this form is by V. Pareto (*op. cit.*, pp. 354–365, 617–657). The details were elaborated by E. Barone ("The Ministry of Production in the Collectivist State," in *Collectivist Economic Planning*, F. A. von Hayek, ed., London: Routledge and Sons, 1935, pp. 245–290). Subsequently, there was a revival and further development by A. P. Lerner ("The Concept of Monopoly and the Measurement of Monopoly Power," *Review of Economic Studies*, Vol. 1, June, 1933, pp. 162–165; see also his *Economics of Control, op. cit.*). A completely rigorous formulation of the results was given by H. Hotelling ("The General Welfare in Relation to Problems of Taxation and Railway Rates," *Econometrica*, Vol. 6, July, 1938, pp. 248–256), and the whole subject is systematically expounded by O. Lange ("The Foundations of Welfare Economics," *op. cit.*, pp. 215–218). It may be remarked that use is made of the maximization methods of the calculus or their graphical equivalents in deriving the result that the maximal alternatives are precisely those states which would be achieved if each individual acted rationally and selfishly in the presence of prices taken as parameters by him. The use of the calculus in these circumstances involves the assumption that each individual consumes some amount of each commodity. The role of this assumption has been pointed out by S. Kuznets in a slightly different context ("On the Valuation of Social Income-Reflections on Professor Hicks' Article," *Economica*, Vol. 15, New Series, February, 1948, pp. 2–6). The theorem in question is valid without the additional assumption; but ordinary calculus methods apparently fail.

a useful preliminary to the analysis of particular social welfare functions, it is hard to see how any policy recommendation can be based merely on a knowledge of the maximal alternatives. There is no way of determining which maximal alternative to decide on; furthermore, even if the current social state is known to be nonmaximal, so that several other alternatives are known to be better than it, there is no way of knowing which of these other alternatives to change to, so that the community will find itself in much the same position as Buridan's ass. There is the less need to discuss the insufficiency of the new welfare economics as a basis for social choice since this point has been argued so well by Professor Samuelson.[5]

However, we may go even further than Samuelson and doubt that any study of maximal alternatives will actually be useful in studying those aspects of social choice which are directly related to consumer's (and worker's) choice. The currently accepted doctrine in this field is that at the social optimum the marginal rate of substitution between two commodities be the same for all consumers. This is derived on the hypothesis that each individual orders social states solely in accordance with the commodities that he receives under each. But it will be shown in Chapter VI that no social welfare function consistent with Conditions 1–5 can be formed if it is assumed that individual orderings of social states are formed in the individualistic manner just sketched, for this is precisely the situation in which the valuations placed on alternative income distributions by different individuals conflict most sharply. That is, the current analysis of maximal social states is applicable precisely when it cannot serve the function of a preliminary to a complete enumeration of the social ordering. This argument will be somewhat qualified in Chapter VI, Section 3.

Of course, a study of maximal social states can be made on other than individualistic assumptions as to the tastes of individuals. But clearly it is necessary first to study the assumptions on individual orderings which will permit the formation of satisfactory social welfare functions before proceeding with the determination of maximal social states.

The same argument does not hold against the corresponding study of the optimum conditions on the production side; but the reason is that these conditions relate to resources whose employment in alternative uses is indifferent to every member of the community except indirectly because of the varying productivity of those resources in the different uses.[6] It is only this assumption that really distinguishes the optimal conditions of production from those of exchange.

[5] *Op. cit.*, pp. 249–252.

[6] Bergson, "A Reformulation . . . ," *op. cit.*, pp. 316–317.

2. The Possibility of Compensation

The compensation principle has been given another meaning first introduced by Mr. Kaldor:[7] In a choice between two alternatives x and y, if there is a method of compensation under state x such that everybody can be made better off in the state resulting from making the compensations under x than they are in y (or everybody can be made at least as well off as in state y and at least one person better off), then x should be chosen above y, *even if the compensation is not actually paid*. It is not contended that the choice pattern dictated by the above rule, which we may term the Kaldor compensation principle, is necessarily optimal from a deeper ethical viewpoint since, of course, it is not precluded that the income distribution prevailing under x might be very unjust indeed. However, Kaldor argues that we can at least say that x is better than y from the viewpoint of aggregate production, leaving the problem of distribution to be settled separately.

The Kaldor compensation principle has been strongly endorsed by Professor Hicks, and criticized by Mr. Baumol.[8] The latter's argument is twofold: (1) the principle carries with it an implicit interpersonal comparison of utility since the potential (but not actual) compensations which are used in the reckoning are measured in money terms, and the social value of a unit of money is therefore reckoned to be the same in the hands of a rich man as in the hands of a poor man; (2) even in the seemingly innocuous case where everybody is actually better off under alternative x than under alternative y, to say that x is better would be valid only in some sort of utilitarian scheme of ethics. The latter point, as has already been seen, is no doubt formally valid in that some sort of value judgment is involved; but the value judgment in question is such a generalized one that we would all be well content to assume it. This is especially so if it is realized that being "better off" may be a function not only of the individual's own consumption, but also of that of others and of the social structure in general, as Baumol himself observes in a footnote.

[7] *Op. cit.*, Chapter I, fn. 9.

[8] Hicks, *op. cit.*, pp. 698–701, 711–712; W. J. Baumol, "Community Indifference," *Review of Economic Studies*, Vol. 14, No. 1, 1946–47, pp. 44–48. Professor Hotelling (*op. cit.*, p. 267) also has suggested application of a principle equivalent to the Kaldor principle but in a much more circumscribed way. It is clear from the context that the situation he envisages is one in which the society to begin with is in a maximal state, as defined in the last section (all prices equal marginal costs), and the choice is between making and not making an indivisible investment, the opportunity for which had not previously existed. In such a case, the Kaldor principle serves merely as a device to keep the economy in a maximal state in the face of changing conditions.

The first objection seems to be somewhat vague. It is true that the results of applying the Kaldor principle would be the same as those of applying the summation-of-utilities criterion when the marginal utility of real income is constant and the same from individual to individual— assuming that the last proviso makes any sense—but this statement is not the same as saying that the Kaldor compensation principle assumes interpersonal comparison of utility. Rather, the Kaldor principle amounts to choosing utility indicators for various individuals' indifference maps according to a rule which makes the marginal utility of income have certain properties; see Chapter III, Section 6. Of course, this means that the principle is arbitrary in the sense that some other rule of choosing utility indicators could have been chosen. For example, instead of finding out from each individual how much of a compensation (positive or negative) each individual would require in state x so that he would be just as well off as in state y and then saying that the community is better off under x than under y if the sum of these compensations is positive, we might find out what fraction (positive or negative) of his income under state x each individual would require to be as well off as in state y and then say that the community is better off under x than under y if the sum of these fractions is positive.[9] The latter rule bears the same relation to the Bernoulli assumption, that the marginal utility of income is inversely proportional to the income, that the Kaldor rule bears to the assumption of constant marginal utility of income. Essentially, Baumol's objection, then, is to the arbitrary nature of Kaldor's principle.

However, even though the Kaldor compensation principle is one of an infinite class, all of which have about the same degree of "reasonableness," it still may be in order to ask if this class at least belongs among the principles for social action which are not to be definitely discarded for some reason. A matter which immediately springs to mind is the desirability of the goal which Kaldor and Hicks set for themselves, that of separating the production aspects of a desired change in social state from the distribution aspects. Any given choice is made on the basis of both considerations; even if a clear-cut meaning were given to an ordering of social states in terms of production, it would not be in the least obvious what use that ordering would be in relation to the desired ordering of social states in terms of all relevant factors, including distributional elements as well as production.

But a deeper objection is that, in a world of more than one commodity, there is no unequivocal meaning to comparing total production in *any* two social states save in terms of some standard of value which makes

[9] This rule has been tentatively suggested by F. Modigliani.

the different commodities commensurable; and usually such a standard of value must depend on the distribution of income. In other words, there is no meaning to total output independent of distribution. In a one-commodity world, i.e., one consumers' good and no labor, of course, the ambiguity disappears, and the Kaldor principle says to maximize the total output of the one commodity.[10] But in general it would appear that, if a state y is discarded and replaced by a state x in accordance with the instructions given by the Kaldor principle, the standard of value used in defining total output is then different from what it formerly was, so that we have, as Baumol says, "a measuring rod which bends, stretches, and ultimately falls to pieces in our hands." [11]

This argument fits well into our formal framework. The Kaldor compensation principle is being proposed as a social welfare function in the sense of Definition 4. Consider the relation $x\,C\,y$, meaning "x is derivable from y by means of compensation payments." For a given set of individual orderings, let R be the corresponding social ordering, P the corresponding social (strict) preference relation (see Definition 1), and Q the unanimity quasi-ordering introduced in the last section. Then Kaldor's principle says that $x\,P\,y$ if there exists an alternative x' such that $x'\,C\,x$, $x'\,Q\,y$, and not $y\,Q\,x'$. It is immediately clear that the Kaldor principle, as stated, violates Condition 3, for, if we do not have both $x\,Q\,y$ and not $y\,Q\,x$, the choice between x and y depends on the relation Q as between some alternatives not in $[x, y]$ and y, and therefore depends on the orderings of individuals for alternatives not in $[x, y]$.

However, we may restate matters in such a way that the Kaldor principle does not violate Condition 3, and I believe this restatement will carry out the meaning of Kaldor and Hicks. The relation C which was introduced may be postulated to have the following properties:

(1)   for all x, $x\,C\,x$;

(2)   for all x and y, $x\,C\,y$ implies $y\,C\,x$;

(3)   for all x, y, and z, $x\,C\,y$ and $y\,C\,z$ imply $x\,C\,z$.

The meaning of these properties is obvious: the first property holds since x can be derived from itself by having everybody pay zero compensation; the second holds since, if x can be derived from y by having individual i pay compensation c_i (positive or negative), then y can be

[10] The assumption of a single commodity has been employed in some of the most illuminating discussions of optimal conditions. See K. Wicksell, *Lectures on Political Economy*, London: G. Routledge and Sons, 1935, Vol. I, p. 140; F. H. Knight, "Fallacies in the Interpretation of Social Cost," in *The Ethics of Competition and Other Essays, op. cit.*, p. 219.

[11] *Op. cit.*, p. 46.

derived from x by having individual i pay compensation $-c_i$; the third holds since, if x can be derived from y by having individual i pay c_i and y from z by having individual i pay c_i', then x can be derived from z by having individual i pay $c_i + c_i'$.

A relation C having properties (1)–(3) is frequently referred to as an *equivalence* or equivalence relation.[12] The relation of indifference is one example of such a relation. As is well known, the indifference relation or any other equivalence can be used to divide the entire original space into mutually exclusive subsets such that each element of any one subset bears the given relation to any other element of that subset, while, if two elements belong to different subsets, the given relation does not hold between them. For example, the indifference relation divides the space of commodity bundles into indifference loci, which have the prescribed properties. In a similar way, the relation C divides all possible social states into mutually exclusive subsets such that $x \, C \, y$ for any x and y in the same subset, while neither $x \, C \, y$ nor $y \, C \, x$ if x and y are not in the same subset.[13] Any one of these subsets may be referred to as a compensatory-equivalent class. The spirit of the Kaldor-Hicks approach is to consider two elements of the same compensatory-equivalent class as being at the same level of production; the choice among such

[12] Tarski, *op. cit.*, pp. 94–96.

[13] A formal proof of this assertion can easily be given. It is required that the totality of social states be divided into subsets having the following properties: (a) every social state is in at least one of the subsets; (b) if x and y are in the same subset, then $x \, C \, y$; (c) if two subsets do not coincide in their entirety, then they are completely disjoint, i.e., either every element of one is an element of the other or the two sets have no elements in common; (d) if x and y are in different subsets, then neither $x \, C \, y$ nor $y \, C \, x$.

We may construct these subsets, or equivalence classes, as we shall call them, as follows: for any given alternative x, let the set of all alternatives x' such that $x' \, C \, x$ be known as the equivalence class generated by x. The equivalence classes generated by all the social states constitute the subsets having the desired properties.

PROOF: (a) By (1), every alternative x is in the equivalence class generated by x.

(b) Let x and y both be in the equivalence class generated by z. Then, by definition, $x \, C \, z$ and $y \, C \, z$. By (2), the second statement implies $z \, C \, y$; from $x \, C \, z$ and $z \, C \, y$ follows $x \, C \, y$ by (3).

(c) Let C_1 and C_2 be two equivalence classes which have an element z in common. Let C_1 be generated by x, and let x' be any element of C_2. By (b), $x' \, C \, z$ and $z \, C \, x$, since z is in both C_1 and C_2; by (3), $x' \, C \, x$, so that x' is in C_1, by definition. Hence, every element of C_2 is in C_1; similarly, every element of C_1 is in C_2, so that C_1 and C_2 coincide in their entirety.

(d) Suppose that x is in C_1, y in C_2, and $x \, C \, y$, where C_1 and C_2 are not entirely coincident. Let C_2 be generated by z; then $y \, C \, z$ by definition, and $x \, C \, z$ by (3), so that x is in C_2 by definition. Then C_1 and C_2 have the element x in common and must, by (c), coincide completely, contrary to hypothesis. Hence, not $x \, C \, y$; by the same reasoning, not $y \, C \, x$.

elements is a question of ethical standards concerning distribution. In line with this, we may imagine a preliminary value judgment as to distribution, selecting from each compensatory-equivalent class one social state which is to be considered admissible. The purpose of the Kaldor principle is then only to rank the admissible alternatives. The other alternatives in any compensatory-equivalent class exist only for the purpose of calculation. Suppose we interpret Condition 3 as requiring only that the choice between any two admissible alternatives be invariant under a change in the individual orderings of other *admissible* alternatives (not necessarily under changes in the individual orderings of nonadmissible alternatives or in the comparisons between nonadmissible and admissible alternatives). Then Condition 3 is satisfied by this restricted form of the Kaldor principle.[14]

But, even with this modification, the social welfare function defined by the Kaldor compensation principle is not compatible with Condition 1, i.e., the social ordering of alternatives generated out of the individual orderings is not even a consistent ranking of those alternatives in the sense of satisfying Axioms I and II. For, as Professor Scitovsky has shown,[15] it is possible under the Kaldor principle that there exists a set of individual orderings such that both $x \, P \, y$ and $y \, P \, x$, a result which is obviously incompatible with the existence of a true social ordering of alternative states.[16]

As stated, Scitovsky's argument is applicable even if there are only two admissible alternatives to rank. That is, there are other logically conceivable alternatives, derived from one or the other of the two given alternatives by a process of compensations, but, as above, a preliminary value judgment as to distribution has removed them from consideration and the only social ordering desired is between the two given alternatives. In the case of two alternatives, however, a simple modification of the Kaldor principle immediately suggests itself for the purpose of removing the contradiction. We may call it the Scitovsky compensation principle; $x \, R \, y$ if and only if there is an alternative x' such that

[14] Of course, the reasoning underlying Condition 3 would be equally applicable to alternatives which are not desired to be ranked; if the choice between any two alternatives is to be independent of tastes for admissible alternatives, then certainly we would wish that choice to be independent of tastes for alternatives which are not even regarded as admissible. We are simply waiving the issue here to get on with other matters.

[15] T. Scitovsky, "A Note on Welfare Propositions in Economics," *Review of Economic Studies*, Vol. 9, November, 1941, pp. 77–88.

[16] That the result, both $x \, P \, y$ and $y \, P \, x$, is incompatible with Axioms I and II can be seen formally as follows: By Definition 1 and Axiom I, $x \, P \, y$ implies not $y \, R \, x$, while $y \, P \, x$ implies $y \, R \, x$, so that both cannot hold simultaneously.

(4) $x' \, C \, x$

and

(5) $x' \, Q \, y.$

We shall assume that, as will usually be the case, for any two alternatives x and y, either there is a method of compensation under x which will make everyone as well off as under y or, if not, there will be a method of compensation under y which will make everyone as well off as under x. This amounts to saying, by (4) and (5), that

(6)   *for all x and y, either $x \, R \, y$ or $y \, R \, x$.*[17]

Since Q is a quasi-ordering, it follows from Definition 7(a) that,

(7)   *for all x, $x \, Q \, x$.*

From (7) and (1), it follows that (4) and (5) are satisfied if both x' and y are equal to x.

(8)   *For all x, $x \, R \, x$.*

Now suppose that $x \, R \, y$ and $y \, R \, z$. Since there are only two alternatives altogether, two of the three alternatives, x, y, and z, must be the same. If $x = y$, then $y \, R \, z$ implies $x \, R \, z$; if $y = z$, then $x \, R \, y$ implies $x \, R \, z$; if $x = z$, then $x \, R \, z$ is equivalent to $x \, R \, x$, which is known to be true by (8).

(9)   *For all x, y, and z, $x \, R \, y$ and $y \, R \, z$ imply $x \, R \, z$.*

By (6) and (9), the relation R defined by the Scitovsky compensation principle is a true weak ordering relation in the case where there are only two admissible alternatives. The relation R is the double test proposed by Scitovsky and accepted by Kaldor;[18] that is, apply the Kaldor principle in those cases where it does not lead to inconsistency; otherwise, say the two alternatives are indifferent.

But the real force of Scitovsky's argument is felt when the number of admissible alternatives becomes more than two, e.g., when the choice is not between free trade and some particular tariff, but the problem is to rank a large number of different possible tariff schedules. Let us

[17] There exist individual orderings of social states based partly on jealousy of the possessions of others for which (6) will not be satisfied for some particular pair x and y.

[18] T. Scitovsky, "A Reconsideration of the Theory of Tariffs," *Review of Economic Studies*, Vol. 9, Summer, 1941, pp. 92–95. "If [the community indifference curves through two given situations] intersect, . . . according to our convention we must regard the two situations as equally good" (pp. 94–95). See also N. Kaldor, "A Comment," *Review of Economic Studies*, Vol. 14, No. 1, 1946–47, p. 49.

consider the Scitovsky compensation principle in this case. If R is really a weak ordering relation, then, by Lemma 1(d), the indifference relation formed from it by Definition 2 is transitive. We shall show by means of an example that Scitovsky indifference is not transitive, and hence that the Scitovsky compensation principle is not a social welfare function satisfying Condition 1. Note that, from (4) and (5), indifference between alternatives x and y means that there is a way of redistributing the goods under x so that everyone is at least as well off as under y and also a way of redistributing the goods under y so that everyone is at least as well off as under x. We will suppose that there are two commodities, two individuals, and three alternative social states, each state being described by giving the amount of each commodity held by each individual under that state. The description is given by the table below. We will assume that each individual orders different social states

Social State	Individual 1		Individual 2	
	Commodity 1	Commodity 2	Commodity 1	Commodity 2
x	2.0	1.0	2.0	1.0
y	1.7	1.3	1.8	1.1
z	1.0	2.0	1.0	2.0

by the commodity bundles he gets under each. Let a commodity bundle be designated by (a, b), where a is the amount of the first commodity in the bundle and b the amount of the second commodity. Suppose that the indifference map of individual 1 is such that the bundles (2.1, 1.0), (1.0, 2.0), (2.4, .7), (1.7, 1.3), and (2.0, 1.0) are preferred in that order and that the indifference curve through the bundle (1.0, 2.0) contains no bundle in which the quantity of the second commodity is less than .9. Similarly, suppose that the indifference map of individual 2 orders the bundles (1.4, 1.4), (1.0, 2.0), (1.6, 1.3), (1.8, 1.1), and (2.0, 1.0) in that order and that the indifference curve through (1.0, 2.0) has no point on it for which the second coordinate is less than 1.2. It can easily be seen that there are indifference maps having the indicated properties in which the indifference curves are continuous, convex, and downward-sloping.

In state y, each individual is better off or not worse off than in state x, so that it is trivial to say that there exists a redistribution of the goods in state y which will make everybody no worse off than in state x.

On the other hand, there are a total of four units of commodity 1 and two of commodity 2 in state x. Suppose we redistribute the quantities in state x as follows: give 2.4 units of commodity 1 and .7 unit of commodity 2 to individual 1 and the remainder, 1.6 units of commodity 1 and 1.3 units of commodity 2, to individual 2. Then both individuals are better off than in state y. Therefore, there is a redistribution of the goods in state x which makes everybody at least as well off as in state y, and hence, by the above definition of Scitovsky indifference, states x and y are indifferent.

By looking at their preference scales, it is clear that both individuals are better off in state z than in state y. On the other hand, there are 3.5 units of commodity 1 in state y and 2.4 units of commodity 2. Redistribute them as follows: (2.1, 1.0) to individual 1 and (1.4, 1.4) to individual 2. Then both individuals are better off than in z. Therefore, again states y and z are indifferent.

It will now be shown that states x and z are not indifferent. It is again obvious that each individual prefers z to x. For individual 1 to be at least as well off as in z, he must have at least .9 unit of the second commodity, while individual 2 must have at least 1.2 units. In any distribution of goods which will make both individuals at least as well off as in state z, there must, then, be a total of at least 2.1 units of the second commodity; but there are only 2 units of the second commodity available in state x. Therefore, every possible redistribution in state x leads to a situation in which at least one individual is worse off than in z, so that x and z are not indifferent, and hence Scitovsky's indifference is not transitive.

The comparison of states x and y illustrates another difficulty with any form of the compensation principle which does not involve actual payments. It is possible for every individual to be better off in one state than another (here, state y as compared with state x), and yet there is a redistribution of the goods in state x so that everybody is no worse off than in the obviously superior state y. This suggests strongly that unaccomplished redistributions are irrelevant.

It is to be noted that the arguments presented here against the compensation principle in its various forms are independent of the contention that that principle involves an undue sanctification of the status quo. The last argument amounts to objecting on ethical grounds to a certain value judgment implicit in the principle, whereas the previous arguments have been to the effect that the value judgments defining the principle were inconsistent with the possibility of rational choice by the community as a whole.

CHAPTER V

THE GENERAL POSSIBILITY THEOREM
FOR SOCIAL WELFARE FUNCTIONS

1. THE NUMBER OF ALTERNATIVES

The discussion of particular social welfare functions in Chapter III, Section 6, and Chapter IV suggests strongly that it will be very difficult to construct a social welfare function consistent with Conditions 1–5. The example of the Scitovsky compensation principle, as given in Chapter IV, Section 2, indicates that there is likely to be a difference between the case where the total number of alternatives to be ranked is two and the case where the number exceeds two. Indeed, if there are two alternatives, it is possible to construct such a social welfare function. Condition 1 must, of course, be altered for this case. We demand now that every set of individual orderings of the two alternatives in question give rise to a social ordering satisfying Axioms I and II.

DEFINITION 9: *By the* method of majority decision *is meant the social welfare function in which $x \, R \, y$ holds if and only if the number of individuals such that $x \, R_i \, y$ is at least as great as the number of individuals such that $y \, R_i \, x$.*

It is not hard to see that the method of majority decision satisfies Conditions 1–5 when there are only two alternatives. To show that it satisfies Condition 1 we must show that R, as defined, is a weak ordering, i.e., is connected and transitive. For convenience, let $N(x, y)$ be the number of individuals such that $x \, R_i \, y$. Then

(1) $$x \, R \, y \text{ if and only if } N(x, y) \geq N(y, x).$$

Clearly, always either $N(x, y) \geq N(y, x)$ or $N(y, x) \geq N(x, y)$, so that,

(2) $$\text{for all } x \text{ and } y, \, x \, R \, y \text{ or } y \, R \, x,$$

by (1), and R is connected. To show transitivity, suppose $x \, R \, y$ and $y \, R \, z$. Since there are only two alternatives, two of x, y, and z are equal. As already shown in the case of the Scitovsky compensation principle, the conclusion $x \, R \, z$ is trivial if $x = y$ or $y = z$. To show $x \, R \, z$ in the case $x = z$ is equivalent to showing $x \, R \, x$. But, by (1), $x \, R \, x$ is equivalent to the proposition $N(x, x) \geq N(x, x)$, and is certainly true. Hence, transitivity holds. In conjunction with (2), this proves that R is a weak ordering, so that

(3)   *the method of majority decision satisfies Condition 1.*

Now consider Condition 2. Let $R_1, \cdots, R_n$ be such that $x \, P \, y$, i.e., $x \, R \, y$ and not $y \, R \, x$. By (1), this means $N(x, y) \geq N(y, x)$ but not $N(y, x) \geq N(x, y)$, i.e.,

(4) $$N(x, y) > N(y, x).$$

Let $R_1', \cdots, R_n'$ be a new set of individual orderings satisfying the hypothesis of Condition 2, i.e., for $x' \neq x$, $y' \neq x$, $x' \, R_i' \, y'$ if and only if $x' \, R_i \, y'$; $x \, R_i \, y'$ implies $x \, R_i' \, y'$; and $x \, P_i \, y'$ implies $x \, P_i' \, y'$. Consider, in particular, the last two conditions with $y' = y$.

(5) $x \, R_i \, y$ *implies* $x \, R_i' \, y$;

(6) $x \, P_i \, y$ *implies* $x \, P_i' \, y$.

Suppose, for some i, $y \, R_i' \, x$. By Definition 1, not $x \, P_i' \, y$, and therefore, by (6), not $x \, P_i \, y$. Hence, by Lemma 1(e), $y \, R_i \, x$. That is,

(7) $y \, R_i' \, x$ *implies* $y \, R_i \, x$.

Let $N'(x, y)$ be the number of individuals for whom $x \, R_i' \, y$; similarly, $N'(y, x)$ is the number of individuals for whom $y \, R_i' \, x$. By (5), every individual for whom $x \, R_i \, y$ has the property $x \, R_i' \, y$; hence, $N'(x, y) \geq N(x, y)$. Similarly, from (7), $N(y, x) \geq N'(y, x)$. From (4), $N'(x, y) > N'(y, x)$ or $N'(x, y) \geq N'(y, x)$ and not $N'(y, x) \geq N'(x, y)$. By (1), this means that $x \, R' \, y$ but not $y \, R' \, x$, where R' is the social ordering corresponding to the set of individual orderings $R_1', \cdots, R_n'$, or $x \, P' \, y$, by Definition 1. Therefore, Condition 2 is satisfied.

Condition 3 (independence of irrelevant alternatives) is trivial in this case because the only set S that contains more than one member contains the entire universe, which consists of two members. If S contains one element, $C(S)$ is that one element independent of tastes about alternatives not in S; if S contains two elements, $C(S)$ is certainly determined by individual orderings for elements in S since there are no others.

As for Condition 4 for any x and y, suppose that individual orderings were such that $y \, P_i \, x$ for all i. Then, for everybody, $y \, R_i \, x$, while, for nobody, $x \, R_i \, y$. Hence, $N(y, x) \geq N(x, y)$ but not $N(x, y) \geq N(y, x)$, so, by (1), $y \, P \, x$, and therefore not $x \, R \, y$, by Definition 1. Hence, we do not have $x \, R \, y$ independent of the individual orderings $R_1, \cdots, R_n$.

Finally, as for Condition 5 (nondictatorship), suppose that there were an individual i satisfying the conditions of Definition 6. Call him 1.

Suppose $x\ P_1\ y$, while $y\ P_i\ x$ for all $i \neq 1$. Then, $x\ R_1\ y$, not $x\ R_i\ y$ for $i \neq 1$, by Definition 1, so that $N(x,\ y) = 1$. Also, $y\ R_i\ x$ for $i \neq 1$, so that $N(y,\ x) \geq 1 = N(x,\ y)$. By (1), $y\ R\ x$, and therefore, by Definition 1, not $x\ P\ y$. By Definition 6, however, $x\ P_1\ y$ implies $x\ P\ y$. Hence there cannot be any dictator, so that Condition 5 is satisfied.

THEOREM 1 (Possibility Theorem for Two Alternatives): *If the total number of alternatives is two, the method of majority decision is a social welfare function which satisfies Conditions 2–5 and yields a social ordering of the two alternatives for every set of individual orderings.*

Theorem 1 is, in a sense, the logical foundation of the Anglo-American two-party system.

For later reference, observe that the proof given above that the method of majority decision satisfies Conditions 2, 4, and 5 was independent of the assumption that there were only two alternatives. It is also true that the method of majority decision satisfies Condition 3 regardless of the total number of alternatives. From Definition 9, it is obvious that the truth or falsity of the statement $x\ R\ y$ is invariant under any change of individual orderings which leaves invariant, for each individual, the relative positions of x and y. By Definition 3, $C(S)$ is completely determined by knowing the truth or falsity of the statement $x\ R\ y$ for every pair x, y of elements of S; hence, $C(S)$ is certainly invariant under any change of the individual orderings which leaves the orderings within S invariant.

LEMMA 3: *For any space of alternatives, the method of majority decision is a social welfare function satisfying Conditions 2–5.*

The example of the paradox of voting given in Chapter I, Section 1, shows that the method of majority decision does not satisfy Condition 1 when there are more than two alternatives. We are now prepared to examine the construction of social welfare functions in this last case.

We shall hereafter assume that Condition 1 holds in its original form.

2. Two Individuals and Three Alternatives

To illustrate the methods of analysis and serve as an introduction to the more general case, we shall consider first the formation of a social welfare function for two individuals expressing their preferences for three alternatives. Some consequences will be drawn from Conditions 1–5. It will be shown that the supposition that there is a social welfare function satisfying those conditions leads to a contradiction.

Let x, y, z be the three alternatives among which choice is to be made, e.g., three possible distributions of commodities. Let x' and y' be variable symbols which represent possible alternatives, i.e., which range over the values x, y, z. Let the individuals be designated as 1 and 2, and let R_1 and R_2 be the orderings by 1 and 2, respectively, of the alternatives x, y, z. Let P_1 and P_2 be the corresponding preference relations; e.g., $x' P_1 y'$ means that individual 1 strictly prefers x' to y'. It is assumed that there is no a priori reason to suppose that the individuals will not order the alternatives in any given way. For example, if it is supposed that each individual values each distribution of commodities in accordance with his preference for his personal share alone (individualistic behavior), if there is more than one commodity, and if no alternative gives any individual more of all commodities than any other alternative, then, by suitable variation of tastes, each individual may order the alternatives in any logically possible manner (see Chapter VI, Section 4, for an example).

CONSEQUENCE 1: *If $x' P_1 y'$ and $x' P_2 y'$, then $x' P y'$.*

That is, if both prefer x' to y', then society must prefer x' to y'.

PROOF: By Condition 4, there are orderings R_1' and R_2' for individuals 1 and 2, respectively, such that, in the corresponding social preference, $x' P' y'$. Form R_1'' from R_1' by raising x', if need be, to the top while leaving the relative positions of the other two alternatives alone; form R_1'' from R_2' in the same way. Since all we have done is raise alternative x' in everyone's esteem while leaving the others alone, x' should still be preferred to y' by society in accordance with Condition 2, so that $x' P'' y'$. But, by construction, both individuals prefer x' to y' in the orderings R_1'', R_2'', and society prefers x' to y'. Since, by Condition 3, the social choice between x' and y' depends only on the individual orderings of those two alternatives, it follows that whenever both individuals prefer x' to y', regardless of the rank of the third alternative, society will prefer x' to y', which is the statement to be proved.

CONSEQUENCE 2: *Suppose that for some x' and y', whenever $x' P_1 y'$ and $y P_2 x'$, $x P' y$. Then, whenever $x' P_1 y'$, $x' P y'$.*

That is, if in a given choice the will of individual 1 prevails against the opposition of 2, then individual 1's views will certainly prevail if 2 is indifferent or if he agrees with 1.

PROOF: Let R_1 be an ordering in which $x' P_1 y'$, and let R_2 be any ordering. Let R_1' be the same ordering as R_1, while R_2' is derived from R_2 by depressing x' to the bottom while leaving the relative positions of the other two alternatives unchanged. By construction, $x' P_1' y'$,

$y' \, P_2' \, x'$. By hypothesis, $x' \, P' \, y'$, where P' is the social preference relation derived from the individual orderings R_1', R_2'. Now the only difference between R_1', R_2' and R_1, R_2 is that x' is raised in the scale of individual 2 in the latter as compared with the former. Hence, by Condition 2 (interchanging the R_i's and the R_i''s), it follows from $x' \, P' \, y'$ that $x' \, P \, y'$. That is, whenever R_1, R_2 are such that $x' \, P_1 \, y'$, then $x' \, P \, y'$.

CONSEQUENCE 3: *If $x' \, P_1 \, y'$ and $y' \, P_2 \, x'$, then $x' \, I \, y'$.*

That is, if the two individuals have exactly opposing interests in the choice between two given alternatives, then society will be indifferent between the alternatives.

PROOF: Suppose the consequence false. Then, for some orderings R_1 and R_2 and for some pair of alternatives x' and y', we would have $x' \, P_1 \, y'$, $y' \, P_2 \, x'$, but not $x' \, I \, y'$. In that case, either $x' \, P \, y'$ or $y' \, P \, x'$. We will suppose $x' \, P \, y'$ and show that this supposition leads to a contradiction; the same reasoning would show that the assumption $y' \, P \, x'$ also leads to a contradiction.

Without loss of generality, it can be assumed that x' is the alternative x, $y' = y$. Then we have, for the particular orderings in question, $x \, P_1 \, y$, $y \, P_2 \, x$, and $x \, P \, y$. Since the social choice between x and y depends, by Condition 3, only on the individual choices as between x and y, we must have

(1)   *whenever $x \, P_1 \, y$ and $y \, P_2 \, x$, $x \, P \, y$.*

It will be shown that (1) leads to a contradiction.

Suppose that individual 1 prefers x to y and y to z, while individual 2 prefers y to z and z to x. Individual 2 then prefers y to x. By (1), society prefers x to y. Also, both prefer y to z; by Consequence 1, society prefers y to z. Since society prefers x to y and y to z, it must prefer x to z. Therefore we have exhibited orderings R_1, R_2 such that $x \, P_1 \, z$, $z \, P_2 \, x$, but $x \, P \, z$. Since the social choice between x and z depends only on the individual preferences for x and z,

(2)   *whenever $x \, P_1 \, z$ and $z \, P_2 \, x$, $x \, P \, z$.*

Now suppose that R_1 is the ordering y, x, z, and R_2 is the ordering z, y, x. By Consequence 1, $y \, P \, x$; by (2), $x \, P \, z$, so that $y \, P \, z$. By the same reasoning as before,

(3)   *whenever $y \, P_1 \, z$ and $z \, P_2 \, y$, $y \, P \, z$.*

If R_1 is the ordering y, z, x, and R_2 is the ordering z, x, y, it follows from Consequence 1 and (3) that $z \, P \, x$ and $y \, P \, z$, so that $y \, P \, x$. Hence,

(4)   *whenever $y \, P_1 \, x$ and $x \, P_2 \, y$, $y \, P \, x$.*

If R_1 is the ordering z, y, x, and R_2 is the ordering x, z, y, then, from Consequence 1 and (4), $z\,P\,y$ and $y\,P\,x$, so that $z\,P\,x$.

(5) $\qquad\qquad$ *Whenever* $z\,P_1\,x$ *and* $x\,P_2\,z$, $z\,P\,x$.

If R_1 is the ordering z, x, y, and R_2 is the ordering x, y, z, then, using (5), $z\,P\,x$ and $x\,P\,y$, so that $z\,P\,y$.

(6) $\qquad\qquad$ *Whenever* $z\,P_1\,y$ *and* $y\,P_2\,z$, $z\,P\,y$.

From (1) it follows from Consequence 2 that, whenever $x\,P_1\,y$, $x\,P\,y$. Similarly, from (1)–(6), it follows that for any pair of alternatives x', y', whenever $x'\,P_1\,y'$, then $x'\,P\,y'$. That is, by Definition 6, individual 1 would be a dictator. This is prohibited by Condition 5, so that (1) must be false. Therefore Consequence 3 is proved.

Now suppose that individual 1 has the ordering x, y, z, while individual 2 has the ordering z, x, y. By Consequence 1,

(7) $\qquad\qquad\qquad\qquad x\,P\,y$.

Since $y\,P_1\,z$, $z\,P_2\,y$, it follows from Consequence 3 that

(8) $\qquad\qquad\qquad\qquad y\,I\,z$.

From (7) and (8), $x\,P\,z$. But also $x\,P\,z$, $z\,P\,x$, which implies $x\,I\,z$ by Consequence 3. It cannot be that x is both preferred and indifferent to z. Hence the assumption that there is a social welfare function compatible with Conditions 1–5 has led to a contradiction.

3. PROOF OF THE GENERAL POSSIBILITY THEOREM

In the following proof we assume a given social welfare function satisfying Conditions 1–5 and show that the assumption leads to a contradiction. Without loss of generality we may suppose that the entire universe is the set of three alternatives mentioned in the statement of Condition 1. In this set, all sets of individual orderings are admissible, so that we need not discuss in each case whether or not a given set is admissible. That is, the orderings which appear in the argument will be orderings only of the three alternatives in question. If we wish to be formally correct and consider the ordering of all alternatives, we can replace each set of orderings of the three given alternatives by a corresponding admissible set of individual orderings which orders the three given alternatives in the same way.

In what follows, V will stand for a set of individuals. In particular, V' will be a set containing a single individual and V'' will be the set of all individuals.

DEFINITION 10: *The set V is said to be decisive for x against y if $x \neq y$ and $x\,P\,y$ for all sets of admissible individual ordering relations such that $x\,P_i\,y$ for all i in V.*

This definition may be explained as follows: Let $\bar{R}$ stand for the set of individual ordering relations $R_1, \cdots, R_n$. The condition $x\,P_i\,y$ for all i in V restricts the $\bar{R}$'s under consideration by restricting the range of variation of those components of $\bar{R}$ whose subscripts are in V to ordering relations having the given property with respect to x and y. To each $\bar{R}$, a given social welfare function assigns a social ordering R; according to this scale we may have, in general, $x\,P\,y$ or $x\,I\,y$ or $y\,P\,x$. Suppose that it so happens that, for all $\bar{R}$ consistent with the condition that $x\,P_i\,y$ for all i in V, the resultant R is such that $x\,P\,y$; then we can say that V is decisive for x against y. Intuitively, the concept of decisive set can be explained as follows: A set of individuals is decisive if, whenever they all prefer x to y, society prefers x to y regardless of what preferences any individuals may have concerning any alternatives other than x or y. Note that a set may be decisive for x against y without being decisive for y against x. For example, in the process of ratification of treaties by the Senate, any set of 64 senators is decisive for acceptance against rejection, any set of 33 senators is decisive for rejection against acceptance.

It should be emphasized that the question of whether or not a given set of individuals is decisive with respect to a given pair of alternatives, x and y, is determined by the social welfare function and does not vary with the actual orderings of individuals at any given time.

CONSEQUENCE 1: *Let $R_1, \cdots, R_n$ and $R_1', \cdots, R_n'$ be two sets of individual orderings such that for a given distinct x and y, $x\,P_i'\,y$ for all i for which $x\,R_i\,y$. Then, if $x\,P\,y$, $x\,P'\,y$, where P and P' are the social preference relations corresponding to $R_1, \cdots, R_n$ and $R_1', \cdots, R_n'$, respectively.*

This consequence extends Condition 2. If x rises or does not fall relative to y for each individual and actually rises if x and y were indifferent, and if x was socially preferred to y to begin with, then x is still preferred to y, regardless of changes in preferences for alternatives other than y.

PROOF: In accordance with the preceding remarks, we assume there are only three alternatives altogether. Let z be the alternative which is distinct from x and y. For each i, define the ordering R_i'', as follows:

(1) $x'\,R_i''\,y'$ *if and only if either* $x'\,R_i\,y'$ *and* $x' \neq z$ *or* $y' = z$.

This amounts to moving z from its position in R_i to the bottom but otherwise leaving R_i unchanged. It is easy to verify that R_i'' is an ordering, i.e., satisfies Axioms I and II. Also, for each i, R_i'' orders the elements x, y in the same way as R_i; i.e.,

(2) $x' R_i'' y'$ if and only if $x' R_i y'$ for x', y' in $[x, y]$.

From (2) and Condition 3, $C([x, y]) = C''([x, y])$, where $C(S)$ and $C''(S)$ are the social choices made from an environment S when $R_1, \cdots, R_n$ and $R_1'', \cdots, R_n''$ are the sets of individual orderings, respectively. By hypothesis, $x P y$; from Lemma 2, $C([x, y])$ contains the single element x. Hence, $C''([x, y])$ contains the single element x, or, by Lemma 2,

(3) $x P'' y$.

Define the individual orderings $R_1^*, \cdots, R_n^*$, as follows:

(4) $x'R_i^* y'$ if and only if either $x' R_i' y'$ and $x' \neq z$ or $y' = z$.

(4) is exactly parallel to (1). From (1), (4), and Definition 1, $y P_i'' z$, $y P_i^* z$, for all i. Hence,

(5)   if $x' \neq x$, $y' \neq x$, $x' R_i'' y'$ if and only if $x' R_i^* y'$.

Also, $x P_i'' z$, $x P_i^* z$ for all i. By (1), for all i such that $x R_i'' y$, $x R_i y$; by hypothesis, $x P_i' y$ for such i, and therefore, by (4), $x P_i^* y$. Hence,

(6)   for all y', $x R_i'' y'$ implies $x R_i^* y'$;

(7)   for all y', $x P_i'' y'$ implies $x P_i^* y'$.

By (5)–(7) and (3), the hypotheses of Condition 2 are satisfied; hence, $x P^* y$. From (4), it follows, in the same manner as above, that $C^*([x, y]) = C'([x, y])$, so that $x P' y$. Q.E.D.

This proof is really simple in principle. The purpose in introducing the auxiliary ordering relations R_i'' and R_i^* was to permit a comparison between the two sets which would satisfy the hypotheses of Condition 2. At the same time, as far as the choice between alternatives x and y is concerned, the relations R_i'' are essentially equivalent to the relations R_i and the relations R_i^* are equivalent to the relations R_i'; this is shown by the latter part of the proof.

CONSEQUENCE 2: *If there is some set of individual ordering relations $R_1, \cdots, R_n$ such that $x P_i y$ for all i in V and $y P_i x$ for all i not in V, for some particular x and y, and such that the corresponding social preference relation yields the outcome $x P y$, then V is decisive for x against y.*

PROOF: Let $R_1', \cdots, R_n'$ be any set of individual orderings subject only to the condition that

(8) $x P_i' y$ for all i in V.

To show that V is decisive, it is necessary according to Definition 10 to show that, for every such set R_1', $\cdots$, R_n', the corresponding social ordering R' is such that $x\,P'\,y$. But from (8) and the hypothesis that $x\,P_i\,y$ for i in V, $y\,P_i\,x$ for i not in V, it follows that $x\,P_i'\,y$ whenever $x\,R_i\,y$. By Consequence 1, $x\,P'\,y$. Q.E.D. The meaning of this consequence may be formulated somewhat as follows: Imagine an observer seeing individuals write down their individual orderings and hand them to the central authorities who then form a social ordering based on the individual orderings in accordance with the social welfare function. Suppose further that this observer notices that, for a specific pair of alternatives x and y, every individual in a certain set V of individuals prefers x to y, while everybody not in V prefers y to x, and that the resultant social ordering ranks x higher than y. Then, the observer is entitled to say, without looking at any other aspects of the individual and social orderings, that V is a decisive set for x against y, i.e., that, if tastes change, but in such a way that all the individuals in V still prefer x to y (though they might have changed their ranking for all other alternatives and though the individuals not in V might have changed their scale completely), then the social ordering will still rank x higher than y.

CONSEQUENCE 3: *For every x and y such that $x \neq y$, V'' is a decisive set for x against y.*

That is, if every individual prefers x to y, then society prefers x to y.

PROOF: If we interchange x and y in Definition 5, then Condition 4 says that there exists a set of individual orderings R_1, $\cdots$, R_n such that not $y\,R\,x$, where R is the social ordering corresponding to the set of individual ordering relations R_1, $\cdots$, R_n. That is to say, by Lemma 1(e),

$$(9) \qquad\qquad x\,P\,y.$$

Let R_1', $\cdots$, R_n' be any set of individual orderings such that

$$(10) \qquad\qquad x\,P_i'\,y \text{ for all } i.$$

From (10), certainly $x\,P_i'\,y$ for all i such that $x\,R_i\,y$. Then, from (9) and Consequence 1, $x\,P'\,y$. Since this holds for any set of orderings satisfying (10), it follows from the definition of V'' that $x\,P'\,y$ for any set of orderings such that $x\,P_i'\,y$ for i in V'', $y\,P_i'\,x$ for i not in V'' (i.e., for no i). By Consequence 2, V'' is decisive for x against y.

CONSEQUENCE 4: *If V' is decisive for either x against y or y against z, V' is decisive for x against z, where x, y, and z are distinct alternatives.*

Recall that V' is a set consisting of a single individual. The consequence asserts that, if a single individual is decisive for a given alternative x against any other alternative, he is decisive for x against any alternative, and that, if he is decisive for any alternative against a given alternative z, he is decisive for any alternative against z. This is the first consequence in which some paradoxes begin to appear.

PROOF: (a) Assume that V' is decisive for x against y. We seek to prove that V' is decisive for x against any $z \neq x$.

Let the individual in V' be given the number 1. Let $R_1, \cdots, R_n$ be a set of individual ordering relations satisfying the conditions

$$(11) \qquad\qquad x\, P_1\, y,$$

$$(12) \qquad\qquad y\, P_i\, z \text{ for all } i,$$

$$(13) \qquad\qquad z\, P_i\, x \text{ for } i \neq 1.$$

From (11), $x\, P_i\, y$ for all i in V'; therefore, by Definition 10,

$$(14) \qquad\qquad x\, P\, y,$$

where P is the social preference relation corresponding to the set of individual orderings $R_1, \cdots, R_n$. From (12), $y\, P_i\, z$ for all i in V''', so that, from Consequence 3 and the definition of a decisive set,

$$(15) \qquad\qquad y\, P\, z.$$

By Condition 1, the social ordering relation satisfies Axioms I and II and hence Lemma 1(c). Therefore, from (14) and (15),

$$(16) \qquad\qquad x\, P\, z.$$

But, from (11) and (12), $x\, P_1\, y$ and $y\, P_1\, z$, so that $x\, P_1\, z$, or

$$(17) \qquad\qquad x\, P_i\, z \text{ for all } i \text{ in } V'.$$

(13) may be written

$$(18) \qquad\qquad z\, P_i\, x \text{ for all } i \text{ not in } V'.$$

By (16)–(18), the hypotheses of Consequence 2 are satisfied, so that V' must be decisive for x against z. That is, there is one set of individual ordering relations in which all the individuals in V' (in this case, one individual) prefer x to z while all other individuals prefer z to x, and the social welfare function is such as to yield a social preference for x as against z. This suffices, by Consequence 2, to establish that V' is decisive for x against z.

(b) Now assume that V' is decisive for y against z. Let the individual in V' have the number 1, and let $R_1, \cdots, R_n$ be a set of individual ordering relations such that

(19) $x \, P_i \, y$ for all i,

(20) $y \, P_1 \, z$,

(21) $z \, P_i \, x$ for $i \neq 1$.

Then, as in part (a) of the proof, (19) implies that $x \, P \, y$, while (20) implies that $y \, P \, z$, so that $x \, P \, z$. But, from (19) and (20), $x \, P_1 \, z$, which, in conjunction with (21), shows that the hypotheses of Consequence 2 are satisfied, and therefore V' is decisive for x against z again.

CONSEQUENCE 5: *For every pair of alternatives x, y and every one-member set of individuals V', it is not true that V' is decisive for x against y.*

This consequence states that no individual can be a dictator for even one pair of alternatives; i.e., there is no individual such that, with the given social welfare function, the community automatically prefers a certain x to a certain y whenever the individual in question does so.

PROOF: Suppose the consequence false. Let the one member of V' be designated by 1.

Let y' be any alternative distinct from x and y. Then, from the hypothesis and Consequence 4, V' is decisive for x against y'. Since this statement is still true for $y' = y$, we may say

(22)   *V' is decisive for x against any $y' \neq x$.*

For a fixed $y' \neq x$, let x' be an alternative distinct from x and y'. This choice is possible by Condition 1 (there are three alternatives). Then, from (22) and Consequence 4, V' is decisive for x' against y'. By (22), this statement still holds if $x' = x$.

(23)   *V' is decisive for x' against y', provided $x' \neq y'$, $y' \neq x$.*

Choose any $x' \neq x$, and a particular y'' distinct from both x and x'. This choice is possible by Condition 1. Then (23) holds; since x', y'', x are distinct, it follows from Consequence 4, if we substitute x' for x, y'' for y, and x for z, that

(24)   *V' is decisive for x' against x, provided $x' \neq x$.*

(23) and (24) together can be written

(25)   *V' is decisive for any x' against any y', provided $x' \neq y'$.*

But, by Definition 10, (25) says that, for all x' and y' (distinct), $x' \, P \, y'$ whenever $x' \, P_1 \, y'$. By Definition 6, this means that the social welfare function is dictatorial, which, however, is excluded by Condition 5. Hence, the supposition that the consequence is false leads to a contradiction with one of the conditions.   Q.E.D.

It will now be shown that Conditions 1–5 lead to a contradiction. Use will be made of the preceding five consequences of the conditions. Let S be the set composed of three distinct alternatives which occurs in the statement of Condition 1. For each possible ordered pair x', y' such that x' and y' both belong to S and $x' \neq y'$ (there are six such ordered pairs), there is at least one set of individuals which is decisive for x' against y' by Consequence 3. Consider all sets of individuals who are decisive for some x' in S against some y', distinct from x', in S. Among these sets, choose the one with the fewest number of individuals; if this condition does not uniquely specify the set, choose any of those decisive sets which does not have more members in it than some other decisive set. For example, if, among all the sets which are decisive for some x' in S against some (distinct) y' in S, there is one with two members and all the others have more than two members, choose that one; on the other hand, if there are two sets decisive for some x' in S against some y' in S which have three members each while all the other decisive sets have more than three members, choose any one of the three-member sets. Designate the chosen set by V_1. It is decisive for some alternative in S against some other one in S; by suitable labeling, we may say that V_1 is decisive for x against y. S contains just one alternative other than x and y; call that alternative z. Let the number of members of V_1 be k; designate the members of V_1 by the numbers $1, \cdots, k$, and number the remaining individuals $k + 1, \cdots, n$. Let V' contain the single individual 1, V_2 the individuals $2, \cdots, k$, and V_3 individuals $k + 1, \cdots, n$. Note that V_3 may contain no members. From the construction of V_1, we may conclude that

(26) V_1 *is decisive for x against y,*

(27)   *any set which is decisive for some alternative in S against some other alternative in S contains at least k members.*

By construction, V_2 contains $k - 1$ members. Hence, from (27),

(28) V_2 *is not decisive for any alternative in S against any other alternative in S.*

Consequence 5 is equivalent to stating that, if V' contains exactly one member, then

(29) V' *is not decisive for any alternative against any other alternative.*

Let $R_1, \cdots, R_n$ be a set of individual ordering relations such that,

(30)   *for i in V', $x\,P_i\,y$ and $y\,P_i\,z$,*

(31)   *for i in V_2, $z\,P_i\,x$ and $x\,P_i\,y$,*

(32)   *for i in V_3, $y\,P_i\,z$ and $z\,P_i\,x$.*

From (30), (31), and the definitions of V_1, V_2, and V', $x\,P_i\,y$ for all i in V_1. From (26),

(33) $x\,P\,y$,

where P is the social preference relation corresponding to $R_1, \cdots, R_n$. From (31), and the fact that R_i is a weak ordering relation and hence transitive,

(34) $z\,P_i\,y$ for all i in V_2.

From (30) and (32),

(35) $y\,P_i\,z$ for all i not in V_2.

Suppose $z\,P\,y$. Then from (34), (35), and Consequence 2, it would follow that V_2 was decisive for y against z; but this contradicts (28). Hence, we must say, not $z\,P\,y$, or

(36) $y\,R\,z$,

where R is the social ordering relation corresponding to $R_1, \cdots, R_n$, the relation from which the preference relation P was derived. By Condition 1, the relation R is a weak ordering relation, having all the usual properties assigned to preference scales, including that of transitivity. Hence, from (33) and (36),

(37) $x\,P\,z$.

From (30), it follows from the transitivity of R_i that

(38) $x\,P_i\,z$ for i in V',

while, from (31) and (32),

(39) $z\,P_i\,x$ for i not in V'.

From (37)–(39) and Consequence 2, it follows that V' is decisive for x against z. But this contradicts (29). Thus, we have shown that Conditions 1–5 taken together lead to a contradiction. Put another way, if we assume that our social welfare function satisfies Conditions 2 and 3 and further suppose that Condition 1 holds, i.e., that there are at least three alternatives which the individuals may order in any way and still get a social ordering, then either Condition 4 or Condition 5 must be violated. Condition 4 states that the social welfare function is not imposed; Condition 5 states that it is not dictatorial.

THEOREM 2 (General Possibility Theorem): *If there are at least three alternatives which the members of the society are free to order in any way, then every social welfare function satisfying Conditions 2 and 3 and yielding a social ordering satisfying Axioms I and II must be either imposed or dictatorial.*[1]

Theorem 2 shows that, if no prior assumptions are made about the nature of individual orderings, there is no method of voting which will remove the paradox of voting discussed in Chapter I, Section 1, neither plurality voting nor any scheme of proportional representation, no matter how complicated. Similarly, the market mechanism does not create a rational social choice.

4. INTERPRETATION OF THE GENERAL POSSIBILITY THEOREM

The interpretation of Theorem 2 is given by examination of the meaning of Conditions 1–5. In particular, it is required that the social ordering be formed from individual orderings and that the social decision between two alternatives be independent of the desires of individuals involving any alternatives other than the given two (Conditions 1 and 3). These conditions taken together serve to exclude interpersonal comparison of social utility either by some form of direct measurement or by comparison with other alternative social states; the arguments in favor of this position have been given in Chapter II, Section 1. Therefore, Theorem 2 can be restated as follows:

If we exclude the possibility of interpersonal comparisons of utility, then the only methods of passing from individual tastes to social preferences which will be satisfactory and which will be defined for a wide range of sets of individual orderings are either imposed or dictatorial.

The word "satisfactory" in the above statement means that the social welfare function does not reflect individuals' desires negatively (Condition 2) and that the resultant social tastes shall be represented by an ordering having the usual properties of rationality ascribed to individual orderings (Condition 1 and Axioms I and II).

[1] The negative outcome expressed in this theorem is strongly reminiscent of the intransitivity of the concept of domination in the theory of multi-person games. (See von Neumann and Morgenstern, *op. cit.*, pp. 38–39.)

In view of the interpretations placed on the conditions for a social welfare function in Chapter III, we can also phrase the result this way: If consumers' values can be represented by a wide range of individual orderings, the doctrine of voters' sovereignty is incompatible with that of collective rationality.

If we wish to make social welfare judgments which depend on the values of all individuals, i.e., which are not imposed or dictatorial, then we must relax some of the conditions imposed. It will continue to be maintained that there is no meaningful interpersonal comparison of utilities and that the conditions wrapped up in the word "satisfactory" are to be accepted.[2] The only condition that remains to be eliminated is the one stating that the method of forming a social ordering should work properly for a wide range of sets of individual orderings. That is, it will now be supposed that it is known in advance that the individual orderings $R_1, \cdots, R_n$ for social actions satisfy certain conditions more restrictive than those permitted in Condition 1, and it is required to find a social welfare function which will be satisfactory for all sets of individual values compatible with those restrictions but not necessarily satisfactory or even defined for other types of individual values. The remaining parts of this essay will be devoted to an examination of the possibilities in this direction.

[2] The only part of the last-named conditions that seems to me to be at all in dispute is the assumption of rationality. The consequences of dropping this assumption are so radical that it seems worth while to explore the consequences of maintaining it. See Chapter II, Section 4.

CHAPTER VI

THE INDIVIDUALISTIC ASSUMPTIONS

1. STATEMENT OF THE ASSUMPTIONS

One important possibility is to impose on the individual preference scales two conditions which in fact have almost invariably been assumed in works on welfare economics: (1) each individual's comparison of two alternative social states depends only on the commodities that he receives (and labor that he expends) in the two states, i.e., he is indifferent as between any two social states in which his own consumption-leisure-saving situations are the same or at least indifferent to him;[1] (2) in comparing two personal situations in one of which he receives at least as much of each commodity (including leisure and saving as commodities) and more of at least one commodity than in the other, the individual will prefer the first situation. However, it can be shown that, in a world of more than one commodity, these restrictions do not suffice to remove the paradox.

The situation we wish to formalize is one in which some but not all of the choices made by an individual are known in advance. Of some pairs x, y it is known that x is preferred to y; of some it is known that x is indifferent to y. This can be reworded by saying that, for some pairs of alternatives, x is known to be preferred or indifferent to y; the case where x is known to be indifferent to y is covered by saying that x is known to be preferred or indifferent to y, and y is known to be preferred or indifferent to x. We assume further that, if x is known to be preferred or indifferent to y but x is not known to be indifferent to y, then x is known to be preferred to y; this is in fact what is found for the true orderings, knowledge for which is given by the individualistic assumptions. The relation of "known preference or indifference" is clearly transitive, but it is not connected since, for example, it does not tell us how the individual compares two social alternatives, one of which yields him more of one commodity than the second, while the second yields him more of a second commodity than the first. On the other hand, we may say certainly that any alternative is known to be preferred

[1] See, e.g., Samuelson, *op. cit.*, pp. 222–224; Bergson, "A Reformulation . . . ," *op. cit.*, pp. 318–320; Lange, "Foundations of Welfare Economics," *op. cit.*, p. 216.

61

or indifferent to itself. Comparison with Definition 7 shows that the relation of "known preference or indifference," as given by the individualistic assumptions, is a quasi-ordering. Furthermore, if, for any individual, R_i is his ordering and Q_i is the quasi-ordering expressing that knowledge about R_i yielded by the individualistic assumptions, then the remarks above, in conjunction with Definition 8, show that R_i must be compatible with Q_i.

Also note that the quasi-ordering of the social alternatives implied in the individualistic assumptions is different for different individuals, since each individual ranks the alternatives involved according to what *he* gets out of them, and an alternative which yields more than a second alternative yields of each commodity to one individual may yield less of each commodity than the second alternative to a second individual.

Formally, we may say that there are n quasi-orderings $Q_1, \cdots, Q_n$, and it is known in advance that the individual ordering relations $R_1, \cdots, R_n$ are compatible with the quasi-orderings $Q_1, \cdots, Q_n$, respectively. If this knowledge is available before we construct our social welfare function, we might feel it superfluous to require that our social welfare function be so defined as to yield a social ordering for a set of individual orderings $R_1, \cdots, R_n$, where, for some i, R_i is not compatible with Q. Hence, Condition 1 can be replaced by the following condition:

CONDITION 1': *The admissible sets of individual ordering relations $R_1, \cdots, R_n$ are precisely those for which R_i is compatible with Q_i for each i.*

2. THE POSSIBILITY THEOREM UNDER INDIVIDUALISTIC ASSUMPTIONS

Clearly, from Theorem 2, Condition 1' will be inconsistent with Conditions 2–5 if the admissible sets of individual orderings are not restricted more sharply by Condition 1' than by Condition 1. Let S be a set of three alternatives about the ordering in which none of the known quasi-orderings tells us anything; i.e., suppose that, for each individual i and for each pair x, y of distinct alternatives in S, not $x Q_i y$. Under the individualistic hypotheses discussed above, an example of such a set would be a set of three alternative distributions of fixed stocks of commodities such that, for each pair of distributions, one gives to any given individual more of one commodity while the second distribution gives more of another commodity.

It is, I think, intuitively clear that restricting the individual orderings to be compatible with the quasi-orderings Q_i is no restriction at all as far as the set S is concerned. Let $T_1, \cdots, T_n$ be any set whatever of n orderings of the set S. For each i, there exists an individual ordering

R_i which is compatible with Q_i and which coincides with T_i on the set S; a rigorous proof of this statement is contained in Lemma 4, proved in the following section. The set of individual orderings $R_1, \cdots, R_n$ is admissible by Condition 1'. But then Condition 1 is satisfied, so Theorem 2 applies, and Conditions 2–5 cannot all be satisfied.

THEOREM 3: *If* $Q_1, \cdots, Q_n$ *are a set of quasi-orderings for which there exists a set S containing at least three alternatives such that, for all i and all x and y in S where x ≠ y, not x Q_i y, then every social welfare function satisfying Condition 1' and Conditions 2 and 3 is either imposed or dictatorial.*

COROLLARY (Possibility Theorem for Individualistic Assumptions): *If there is more than one commodity and if every set of individual orderings each of which satisfies the individualistic assumptions is admissible, then every social welfare function satisfying Conditions 2 and 3 is either imposed or dictatorial.*

Although the motivation for developing Theorem 3 was the analysis of the individualistic case, the conclusion is applicable to any attempt to restrict the range of individual orderings by requiring them to be consistent with any preassigned partial orderings. Thus, if we had modified the previous individualistic ordering by saying that, between two alternatives which yielded the same commodity bundle to a given individual, the individual was not indifferent but chose on the basis of some measure of income equality, while, however, he still preferred any alternative which gave him at least as much of all commodities and more of at least one, the above negative conclusions as to the possibility of a social welfare function would still be applicable, since we could still form the set S which would satisfy the hypotheses of Theorem 3.

The corollary casts light on the usefulness of the analysis of maximal states, as discussed in Chapter IV, Section 1, if we make the assumption that individual desires for social alternatives are formed in the individualistic way discussed in this chapter. If the only restrictions that we wish to impose on individual tastes are those implied by the individualistic assumptions, then no satisfactory social welfare function is possible. Since, as we have seen, the only purpose of the determination of the maximal states is as a preliminary to the study of social welfare functions, the customary study of maximal states under individualistic assumptions is pointless. There is, however, a qualification which should be added. It is conceivable that, if further restrictions are added to the individualistic ones, a social welfare function will be possible; indeed, an example will be given in Chapter VII, Section 2. Any state which is maximal under the combination of individualistic and other restrictions will certainly be maximal if only individualistic restrictions are imposed on the individual orderings. Hence, if the proper handling of the social welfare problem is deemed to be the imposition of further restrictions in addition to the individualistic ones, then the social maximum in any given situation will be one of the maximal elements under the combined restrictions and hence one of the maximal elements under individualistic conditions. It is therefore not excluded that the current new welfare economics will be of some use in restricting the range in which we must look for the social maximum.

3. Quasi-orderings and Compatible Weak Orderings

A lemma with regard to quasi-orderings and weak orderings compatible with them will be proved in this section (see Definitions 7 and 8). The following theorem is equivalent to one of E. Szpilrajn's.[2]

Szpilrajn's Theorem: *If Q is a quasi-ordering, then there is a weak ordering R which is compatible with Q.*

Thus, in ordinary demand theory, we may establish a quasi-ordering among all commodity bundles by saying that a bundle all of whose components are larger than another is superior to it. Szpilrajn's theorem tells us that it is possible to construct a complete indifference map in which the comparisons of such pairs of bundles will satisfy this condition; i.e., we can construct an indifference map with downward-sloping indifference curves. The theorem is trivial in any particular application; nevertheless, it is not trivial in its full generality.

From Szpilrajn's theorem, we will deduce the following lemma.

Lemma 4: *Let Q be a quasi-ordering, S a set of alternatives such that, if $x \neq y$ and x and y both belong to S, then not $x Q y$, and T a relation which establishes a weak ordering on S. Then there is a weak ordering R of all alternatives compatible with Q such that $x R y$ if and only if $x T y$ for x and y in S.*

This means the following: Suppose that, of all possible pairs of alternatives, the choices among some pairs are fixed in advance, and in a consistent way, so that if x is fixed in advance to be chosen over y and y fixed in advance to be chosen over z, then x is fixed in advance to be chosen over z. Suppose, however, that there is a set S of alternatives such that the choice between no pair of them is prescribed in

---

[2] E. Szpilrajn, "Sur l'extension de l'ordre partiel," *Fundamenta Mathematicae*, Vol. 16, 1930, pp. 386–389. I am indebted for this reference to J. C. C. McKinsey.

advance. Then the lemma states that, given *any* ordering of the elements in S, there is a way of ordering all the alternatives which will be compatible both with the given ordering in S and with the choice made in advance. In other words, if we know there is some ordering and we know some of the choices implied by that ordering but the known choices do not give any direct information as to choices between elements in a subset S, then there is also no indirect information as to the choices in S, i.e., the ordering of all the alternatives is compatible with any ordering in S.

Thus, to continue with the example of demand theory, suppose we have, as before, the quasi-ordering implied by the condition that all marginal utilities are positive. Such a quasi-ordering tells us nothing directly about the ordering of the bundles on a given budget plane (assuming positive prices). Lemma 4 tells us, then, that no information whatever is conveyed as to the choice from a given budget plane by the assumption that all marginal utilities are positive; any ordering of the bundles on a given budget plane can be extended to an indifference map for all bundles which can be represented by a utility function all of whose partial derivatives are positive. (Of course, the assumption that marginal utilities are positive does tell us that the choice will be made on the budget plane and not below it.)

PROOF: Let Q'' be any quasi-ordering such that,

(1) $\qquad$ *for all x and y, $x\,Q\,y$ implies $x\,Q''\,y$,*

(2) $\qquad$ *for all x and y in S, $x\,T\,y$ implies $x\,Q''\,y$.*

The relation of universal indifference, i.e., $x\,Q''\,y$ for all x and y, is a quasi-ordering and satisfies (1) and (2), so that there is at least one Q'' satisfying (1) and (2). Define a relation Q' as follows:

(3) $\quad$ $x\,Q'\,y$ *if and only if $x\,Q''\,y$ for all quasi-orderings Q'' satisfying (1) and (2).*

Since each Q'' is a quasi-ordering, it follows from (3) and Definition 7 that

(4) $\qquad\qquad$ Q' *is a quasi-ordering.*

From (1)–(3),

(5) $\qquad$ *for all x and y, $x\,Q\,y$ implies $x\,Q'\,y$,*

(6) $\qquad$ *for all x and y in S, $x\,T\,y$ implies $x\,Q'\,y$.*

Suppose, for some particular x' and y' in S, not $x'\,T\,y'$. Let X_1 be the set of all alternatives x such that either

(7) $$x \text{ in } S, x\, T\, y'$$

or

(8) $$\text{for some } z \text{ in } S, x\, Q\, z \text{ and } z\, T\, y'.$$

Let Q_1 be defined as follows:

(9) $$x\, Q_1\, y \text{ if and only if either } x \text{ in } X_1 \text{ or } y \text{ not in } X_1.$$

It follows from (9) and Definition 7 that

(10) $$Q_1 \text{ is a quasi-ordering.}$$

Suppose, for some x and y, $x\, Q\, y$ and y in X_1. Then, from (7) and (8), either y in S, $y\, T\, y'$, in which case x is in X_1 by (8), or, for some z, $y\, Q\, z$, z in S, $z\, T\, y'$. In the latter case, $x\, Q\, y$ and $y\, Q\, z$ imply $x\, Q\, z$, since Q is a quasi-ordering, so that again x is in X_1 by (8). Hence, in any case, if $x\, Q\, y$ and y is in X_1, then x is in X_1. From (9),

(11) $$x\, Q\, y \text{ implies } x\, Q_1\, y.$$

Now suppose, for some x and y in S, $x\, T\, y$, y in X_1. Then, either $y\, T\, y'$, in which case $x\, T\, y'$, since T is a weak ordering, and therefore x is in X_1 by (7), or $y\, Q\, z$, z in S, $z\, T\, y'$. But since both y and z are in S, the latter can hold only if $y = z$ by hypothesis, and we have $y\, T\, y'$, which is the previous case. As above,

(12) $$\text{for } x \text{ and } y \text{ in } S, x\, T\, y \text{ implies } x\, Q_1\, y.$$

From (10)–(12), Q_1 is a quasi-ordering satisfying (1) and (2). But, from (7), y' belongs to X_1, since $y'\, T\, y'$. Since, by assumption, not $x'\, T\, y'$, (7) cannot hold for $x = x'$. If x' belongs to X_1, then (8) must hold, i.e., $x'\, Q\, z$, z in S, $z\, T\, y'$; but, since x' and z both belong to S, we must have $z = x'$, so that $x'\, T\, y'$, contrary to assumption. Hence, x' does not belong to X_1, so that not $x'\, Q_1\, y'$. From (3), not $x'\, Q'\, y'$. Replacing x' by x and y' by y, we have,

(13) $$\text{for } x \text{ and } y \text{ in } S, \text{ not } x\, T\, y \text{ implies not } x\, Q'\, y.$$

Now suppose, for some particular x' and y', $x'\, Q\, y'$ and not $y'\, Q\, x'$. Let X_2 be the set of all alternatives x such that one of the following holds:

(14) $$x\, Q\, x',$$

(15) $$x \text{ in } S \text{ and, for some } z \text{ in } S, x\, T\, z, z\, Q\, x',$$

(16) $$\text{for some } z_1 \text{ and } z_2 \text{ in } S, x\, Q\, z_1, z_1\, T\, z_2, z_2\, Q\, x'.$$

Define the relation Q_2 as follows:

(17) $x\, Q_2\, y$ *if and only if either x in X_2 or y not in X_2.*

From (17) and Definition 7,

(18) Q_2 *is a quasi-ordering.*

Suppose, for some x and y, $x\, Q\, y$, y in X_2. One of (14)–(16) must hold, with x replaced by y. If $y\, Q\, x'$, then $x\, Q\, x'$, so that x is in X_2. If y in S, z in S, $y\, T\, z$, $z\, Q\, x'$, then x is in X_2 by (16). If $y\, Q\, z_1$, $z_1\, T\, z_2$, $z_2\, Q\, x'$, then, since $x\, Q\, y$, we have $x\, Q\, z_1$, $z_1\, T\, z_2$, $z_2\, Q\, x'$, so x is in X_2 by (16). Hence, as before,

(19) $x\, Q\, y$ *implies* $x\, Q_2\, y$.

Suppose, for some x and y in S, $x\, T\, y$, y in X_2. If $y\, Q\, x'$, then x is in X_2 by (15). If $y\, T\, z$, $z\, Q\, x'$, then, since $x\, T\, y$, $x\, T\, z$, $z\, Q\, x'$, so x is in X_2 by (15). If $y\, Q\, z_1$, $z_1\, T\, z_2$, $z_2\, Q\, x'$, z_1 and z_2 in S, then, since both y and z_1 are in S, $y = z_1$ by hypothesis, so this reduces to the previous case as $y\, T\, z_2$.

(20)   *If x and y are in S, $x\, T\, y$ implies $x\, Q_2\, y$.*

If y' had belonged to X_2, one of (14)–(16) would have held, with $x = y'$. Since not $y'\, Q\, x'$ by assumption, (14) cannot hold. If y' and z in S, $y'\, T\, z$, $z\, Q\, x'$, then, since $x'\, Q\, y'$ by assumption, $z\, Q\, y'$, so that $z = y'$ by the hypothesis about S, and $y'\, Q\, x'$, contrary to assumption. If $y'\, Q\, z_1$, $z_1\, T\, z_2$, $z_2\, Q\, x'$, z_1 and z_2 in S, then $z_2\, Q\, y'$ since $x'\, Q\, y'$, and therefore $z_2\, Q\, z_1$. This implies $z_1 = z_2$, so that $y'\, Q\, z_1$, $z_1\, Q\, x'$, and therefore $y'\, Q\, x'$, contrary to assumption. Therefore, y' does not belong to X_2; on the other hand, x' belongs to X_2 by (14) since $x'\, Q\, x'$. Therefore, not $y'\, Q_2\, x'$, by (17). From (18)–(20) and (1)–(3), not $y'\, Q'\, x'$. Replacing x' by x and y' by y, we get

(21) $x\, Q\, y$ *and not* $y\, Q\, x$ *imply not* $y\, Q'\, x$.

From (4) and Szpilrajn's theorem, there is a weak ordering R of all alternatives such that

(22) R *is compatible with Q'.*

From (5), (22), and Definition 8(c),

(23) $x\, Q\, y$ *implies* $x\, R\, y$.

From (5), (21), (22), and Definition 8(d), $x\, Q\, y$ and not $y\, Q\, x$ imply $x\, Q'\, y$ and not $y\, Q'\, x$, which in turn imply not $x\, R\, y$.

(24) $x\, Q\, y$ *and not* $y\, Q\, x$ *imply not* $x\, R\, y$.

From (23), (24), and Definition 8,

(25)   *R is compatible with Q.*

From (6), (22), and Definition 8(c),

(26)   *for x and y in S, x T y implies x R y.*

Suppose x and y in S and not $x\ T\ y$. Then $y\ T\ x$, since T is a weak ordering. From (6) and (13), $y\ Q'\ x$ and not $x\ Q'\ y$; from (22) and Definition 8(d), not $x\ R\ y$. Combining with (26) shows that,

(27)   *for x and y in S, x R y if and only if x T y.*

(25) and (27) establish the lemma.

4. AN EXAMPLE

Suppose that among the possible alternatives there are three, none of which gives any individual at least as much of both commodities as any other. For example, suppose that there are two individuals and a total of ten units of each of two commodities. Consider three alternative distributions described by the table below. The individualistic

Alternative	Individual 1		Individual 2	
	Commodity 1	Commodity 2	Commodity 1	Commodity 2
1	5	1	5	9
2	4	2	6	8
3	3	3	7	7

restrictions imposed do not tell us anything about the way either individual orders these alternatives. All preferences are permitted, so that we are essentially back in the original situation of unrestricted choice where the paradox holds.

In fact, the same example shows that even further restrictions that have sometimes been used will not suffice. Thus, in the individualistic case, it is occasionally further assumed, at least as a basis for welfare statements, that all men have the same preferences in regard to their individual situations. Given any ordering of the various social alternatives by the two individuals, we can construct a preference scale for the six individual situations involved by assuming the three available to individual 2 to be ranked according to his preferences and all to be superior to the three individual situations available to individual 1, the last being ranked among themselves in accordance with individual 1's tastes. If each allocation of each commodity in alternative 2 is reduced by .5, it is even possible to embed this last preference scale for the individual situations into an indifference map with convex indifference curves; so even assuming convexity does not impose enough restriction on individual preference scales to permit a satisfactory social welfare function.

The results of this section suggest strongly that the difficulties in forming a social welfare function arise from the differing social attitudes which follow from the individualistic hypothesis, especially in the case of similar tastes for individual consumption. It follows that the possibility of social welfare judgments rests upon a similarity of attitudes toward social alternatives.

5. A ONE-COMMODITY WORLD

The insufficiency of the individualistic hypotheses to permit the formation of a social welfare function, as developed in the previous sections, hinged on the assumption that there was more than one commodity involved. An investigation of the one-commodity case may be of interest in bringing out more clearly the issues involved.

In a one-commodity world, if we impose Conditions 1 and 2 of Section 1, there is for any given individual only one possible ordering of the social states. He orders various social states solely according to the amount of the one commodity he gets under each. In such a situation, the individual orderings are not variables; Conditions 2, 3, and 4 become irrelevant since they relate to the variation in the social ordering corresponding to certain specified types of changes in the individual orderings. Condition 5 (nondictatorship) becomes a much weaker restriction, though not completely irrelevant. Any specification of a social ordering which does not coincide completely with the ordering of any one individual will be a social welfare function compatible with all the conditions. For example, for each fixed total output, we might set up arbitrarily an ordering of the various distributions; we then order any two social states with different total outputs in accordance with the total output, any two social states with the same total output according to the arbitrary ordering. This sets up a genuine weak ordering which does not coincide with the ordering of any one individual. For example, let x and y be two states with total outputs s and t, respectively, and with apportionments s' and t', respectively, to the given individual. If $s > t$, but $s' < t'$, then society prefers x to y, while the individual prefers y to x.

The qualitative nature of the difference between the single- and multi-commodity cases makes any welfare arguments based on an implicit assumption of a single commodity dubious in its applicability to real situations. The fundamental difficulty is the same as that pointed out in connection with the Kaldor compensation principle in Chapter IV, Section 2: as soon as more than one commodity exists, there is the question of making them commensurable, i.e., of introducing a standard of values.

6. Group Choice in the Theory of Games

In the present development of the theory of multi-person games, an important role is played by the assumption that each possible coalition ranks all possible alternative strategies according to the sum of the payments to its members.[3] It may be asked why this group choice function does not run into the paradox discussed here. It is true that it is assumed in the theory of games that each individual is playing for his own interests;[4] but it has already been pointed out (see Section 2) that the individualistic hypothesis is insufficient to yield a satisfactory social welfare function.

The world of the theory of games is a one-commodity world, but the situation is somewhat more complicated than that envisaged in the previous section. If there are a number of different possible money payments, any probability distribution over this range is also the outcome to an individual of a possible social alternative (imputation), and each individual ranks not only money payments but also probability distributions of money payments. If no other restriction were imposed, the probabilities of different outcomes would act like different commodities, and the situation of Section 2 would appear. However, Professors von Neumann and Morgenstern assume for the purposes of the theory that individuals rank probability distributions solely according to the expected value of the money return; this ranking is implicit in the assumption of a transferable utility.[5] Again, therefore, the ranking by each individual of alternative social states is prescribed in advance, and the situation is that of the preceding section.

---

[3] Von Neumann and Morgenstern, *op. cit.*, p. 264. The above remark is implicit in the definitions of effective set and domination.

[4] *Ibid.*, pp. 8–9.

[5] *Ibid.*, pp. 604, 629 fn.

7. DISTRIBUTIONAL ETHICS COMBINED WITH INDIVIDUALISM

We may examine briefly a set of assumptions about individual values which seems to be common to those who feel that the new welfare economics is applicable in a fairly direct way to the solution of specific economic problems. It is assumed that there are: (1) an accepted (let us say, unanimously accepted) value judgment that if everybody is better off (more precisely, if everybody is at least as well off and one person better off) in one social state than another *according to his tastes*, then the first social state is preferred to the second; and (2) a universally accepted ordering of different possible welfare distributions in any given situation. The latter value judgment usually takes an egalitarian form.

This ethical scheme is quite explicit in the work of Professor Bergson; the second value judgment is contained in his Propositions of Relative Shares.[6] The same set of ethics underlies the compensation principle of Mr. Kaldor and Professor Hicks; we have already observed the difficulties with that approach (Chapter IV, Section 2). More recently, some proposals made by Professors Johnson and Modigliani for meeting the problem of the increased cost of food due to European demand seem to have been based on value judgments (1) and (2) above.[7] To prevent the inequitable shift in real income to farmers, it was proposed that there be imposed an excise tax on food, accompanied by a per capita subsidy to consumers. Under the assumption that the supply of agricultural goods is completely inelastic, the tax would be absorbed by the farmers while the subsidy would have no substitution effects at the margin, so that the marginal rate of substitution for any pair of commodities would be the same for all consumers and hence the first value judgment would be fulfilled. The taxes and subsidies perform a purely distributive function and can be so arranged as to restore the status quo ante as nearly as may be desired, though actually the payment of a per capita subsidy implies a certain equalizing effect.

The value judgments are assumed here to hold for any individual. Note that to even state these judgments we must distinguish sharply between values and tastes (see Chapter II, Section 3). All individuals are assumed to have the same values at any given instant of time, but the values held by any one individual will vary with variations in the tastes of all. Our previous arguments as to the nonexistence of social

---

[6] Bergson, "A Reformulation . . . ," *op. cit.*, pp. 320–321.

[7] D. Gale Johnson, "The High Cost of Food—A Suggested Solution," *Journal of Political Economy*, Vol. 56, February, 1948, pp. 54–57. Professor Modigliani's proposals are contained in a press release of the Institute of World Affairs, New York, October, 1948.

welfare functions were based, on the diversity of values; do they carry over to this particular kind of unanimity?

The actual distribution of welfare dictated by the second value judgment cannot be stated simply in money terms. As Professor Samuelson points out, such a value judgment is not consistent with any well-defined social ordering of alternative social states.[8] The distribution of real income, for a given environment, must vary with individual tastes. Thus, for a given set of individual tastes (as represented by the ordering relations of all individuals, each for his own consumption) and a given environment, there is a given distribution of purchasing power (somehow defined); then exchange under perfectly competitive conditions proceeds until an optimum distribution is reached. The given distribution of real income and the individual tastes uniquely determine the final outcome, which is a social state. Therefore, the given ethical system is a rule which defines the social state chosen from a given environment as a function of the tastes of all individuals. If, for a given set of tastes, the environment varies, we expect that the choices will be consistent in the sense that the choice function is derivable from a social weak ordering of all social states. Thus, the ethical scheme discussed in this section, which we may term the Bergson social welfare function, has the form of a rule assigning a social ordering to each possible set of individual orderings representing tastes. Mathematically, the Bergson social welfare function has, then, the same form as the social welfare function we have already discussed, though, of course, the interpretation is somewhat different in that the individual orderings represent tastes rather than values, and the whole function is the end product of certain values assumed unanimously held rather than a method of reconciling divergent value systems. If the range of tastes is not restricted by a priori considerations (except that they must truly be tastes, i.e., they must refer only to an individual's own consumption, however that may be defined), then indeed the Bergson social welfare function is mathematically isomorphic to the social welfare function under individualistic assumptions. Hence, the Possibility Theorem under Individualistic Assumptions (Corollary to Theorem 3) is applicable here; we cannot construct a Bergson social welfare function, i.e., one satisfying value judgments (1) and (2), that will satisfy Conditions 2–5 and that will yield a true social ordering for every set of individual tastes. Essentially, the two value judgments amount to erecting individualistic behavior into a value judgment; it is not surprising, then, that such ethics can be no more successful than the actual practice of individualism in permitting the formation of social welfare judgments.

[8] Samuelson, *op. cit.*, p. 225.

It must, of course, be recognized that the meaning of Conditions 2–5 has changed. The previous arguments for their validity assumed that the individual orderings represented values rather than tastes. It seems obvious that Conditions 2, 4, and 5 have the same intrinsic desirability under either interpretation. Condition 3 is perhaps more doubtful. Suppose that there are just two commodities, bread and wine. A distribution, deemed equitable by all, is arranged, with the wine-lovers getting more wine and less bread than the abstainers. Suppose now that all the wine is destroyed. Are the wine-lovers entitled, because of that fact, to more than an equal share of bread? The answer is, of course, a value judgment. My own feeling is that tastes for unattainable alternatives should have nothing to do with the decision among the attainable ones; desires in conflict with reality are not entitled to consideration, so that Condition 3, reinterpreted in terms of tastes rather than values, is a valid value judgment, to me at least.

CHAPTER VII

SIMILARITY AS THE BASIS OF SOCIAL WELFARE JUDGMENTS

1. COMPLETE UNANIMITY

Suppose that we do not assume in advance the shape of the preferences of any one individual, but we do assume that all individuals have the same preferences for social alternatives. This implies a social-minded attitude and also a homogeneous society. If we consider the preferences in question to refer not to expressed preferences but to the preferences which would be expressed if the corruptions of the environment were removed, the assumption of unanimity is the idealist view of political philosophy.[1] In this case, the obvious way of defining the social welfare function is to choose some one individual and then say that the social preference scale shall be the same as his. This satisfies all the conditions set forth in Chapter III except the condition that the social welfare function not be dictatorial. Under the assumptions of this section, since it makes no difference who is dictator, the condition of nondictatorship loses its intrinsic desirability.

We may generalize somewhat. Suppose it is assumed in advance that a majority of the individuals will have the same ordering of social alternatives; it is immaterial whether the particular membership of the majority is known in advance or not. Then the method of majority decision (see Definition 9) will pick out this agreed-on ordering and make it the social ordering. Again all the conditions laid down in Chapter III will be satisfied.

These results, which are trivial from the mathematical point of view, reinforce the suggestion at the end of Chapter VI, Section 4, that like attitudes toward social alternatives (not like tastes for individual consumption) are needed for the formation of social judgments. Some values which might give rise to such similarity of social attitudes are the desires for freedom, for national power, and for equality;[2] likeness

---

[1] See Section 3.

[2] These are here considered as ends in themselves; they also have an instrumental significance in furthering or hindering other ends, and an individual who favors equality, for example, as an end in itself may nevertheless favor a certain amount of inequality in order to increase total output.

in individual tastes, by its very nature, leads to likeness in desires for social alternatives. Somewhat less direct in its social implication is the desire for prolongation of life, which we may take to be one of the most universal of all human motives. This desire is essentially individualistic, extending to only a few individuals at most; but, since the means for achieving increased longevity are in such large part social, there is a strong factor making for like attitudes on special issues. Differences may still arise owing to imperfect knowledge.[3] Of like nature are the various types of collective consumption.

2. THE CASE OF SINGLE-PEAKED PREFERENCES

A radical restriction on the range of possible individual orderings has been proposed recently by Professor Duncan Black.[4] He assumes that, if $U_1, \cdots, U_n$ are utility indicators for the individual orderings $R_1, \cdots, R_n$, then the alternative social states can be represented by a one-dimensional variable in such a way that each of the graphs of $U_1, \cdots, U_n$ has a single peak. An example in which this assumption

---

[3] F. G. Dickinson, of the American Medical Association, has suggested orally that the prolongation of life could itself be used as a social welfare guide. This view is especially attractive since the greater part of social, and particularly economic, activity is devoted to that end, broadly construed. In contrast to other basic motives, such as sex and prestige, the desire for longevity is socializing rather than divisive, although, if one considers the world as one unit, the relation between population and food supply is probably such that strong elements of conflict remain. However, life cannot be taken as a sole objective since, for most human beings, there are specific situations in which human beings are willing to give up their lives in the pursuit of other values, whether these be the aggrandizement of the political unit to which one owes obedience ("Dulce et decorum est pro patria mori"— Horace) or the desire for freedom ("It is better to die on your feet than to live on your knees" —Dolores Ibarruri). From a more practical viewpoint, longevity is probably too insensitive to short-run economic adjustments to serve as a meaningful guide, especially in view of the great uncertainty existing as to the factors making for prolongation of life.

The very measurement of length of life for a whole society involves most of the ambiguities already found in economic welfare analysis. Thus, in evaluating the relative importance of different causes of death, simple death rates have been objected to on the grounds that they ignore age at death, which should be considered since it determines the loss to society occasioned by the death. Therefore, new measures are proposed which seek, at least to a rough approximation, to measure the economic loss to society occasioned by the deaths due to each cause. (See F. G. Dickinson and E. L. Welker, *What Is the Leading Cause of Death? Two New Measures*, Bulletin 64, Bureau of Medical Economic Research, American Medical Association, Chicago, 1948.) Of course, carried to its logical conclusion, this course involves all the difficulties already encountered in ascribing a meaning to social productivity.

[4] See fn. 17, Chapter I.

is satisfied is the party structure of prewar European parliaments, where there was a universally recognized Left-Right ordering of the parties. Individuals might have belonged to any one of the parties; but each recognized the same arrangement, in the sense that, of two parties to the left of his own, the individual would prefer the program of the one less to the left, and similarly with parties on the right. Nothing need be specified as to the relative choice between a party to the right and a party to the left of an individual's first choice.

It is possible to find economic examples in which Black's postulate may be expected to be satisfied. Thus, suppose that, for reasons of technological efficiency, it is required that all workers work the same number of hours, and it is desired to fix the number of hours to be worked. If we assume that wages are to be paid in accordance with marginal productivity, the real wage rate is a known decreasing function of the number of hours selected; hence each social alternative is completely specified by a single number, the number of hours worked. For each individual, the relation between wages and hours worked defines an income-leisure transformation curve. Under individualistic assumptions, we may assume that individuals rank different numbers of hours to be worked by considering the corresponding points on the income-leisure transformation curve and comparing the income-leisure indifference curves which pass through them. We may reasonably suppose that there is one point on the transformation curve for which the individual's utility is maximized and that the individual's utility decreases as the number of hours worked varies in either direction from the optimum. Then Black's postulate is satisfied.

Black shows that, under his assumption of single-peaked preferences, the method of majority decision (see Definition 9) will lead to determinate results, since there is exactly one alternative which will receive a majority over any other, provided the number of voters is odd.[5] If the total number of alternatives is finite, this result shows that, for any set of individual orderings representable by single-peaked preferences, the method of majority decision leads to a transitive ordering of the alternatives; for we may remove the best alternative and then consider the one that is best among the remainder, in the sense of being preferred by a majority of the individuals to any other alternative left, as being second-best, etc.[6] However, the proof in the general case of any number of alternatives requires other methods. Let us therefore redefine the assumption of single-peaked preferences in a formal way.

---

[5] Black, "On the Rationale . . . ," *op. cit.*, pp. 26–28; "Decisions of a Committee . . . ," *op. cit.*, pp. 250–251.

[6] Black, "On the Rationale . . . ," *op. cit.*, p. 30.

Under this assumption, there is a way of ordering the alternatives so that each individual ordering will be representable by a single-peaked utility curve. This basic reordering of the alternative social states is not a weak ordering of the type defined by Axioms I and II since, of any two distinct alternatives, one must precede the other. Such an ordering is analogous to the relation of "less than" in the domain of real numbers; we may call it a strong ordering.

DEFINITION 11: *The relation S is said to be a strong ordering relation if,*
(a) *for all x, not $x\,S\,x$;*
(b) *for all $x \neq y$, either $x\,S\,y$ or $y\,S\,x$;*
(c) *for all x, y, and z, $x\,S\,y$ and $y\,S\,z$ imply $x\,S\,z$.*

In terms of a strong ordering, we can define the concept of "betweenness" in an obvious way. Let $B(x, y, z)$ mean "y is between x and z."

DEFINITION 12: *If S is a strong ordering, define $B(x, y, z)$ to mean that either $x\,S\,y$ and $y\,S\,z$ or $z\,S\,y$ and $y\,S\,x$.*

An obvious consequence of Definitions 11 and 12 is the following lemma.

LEMMA 5: *If x, y, z are distinct, then one and only one of the following holds: $B(x, y, z)$, $B(y, x, z)$, $B(y, z, x)$.*

Black's assumption may be written as follows.

ASSUMPTION OF SINGLE-PEAKED PREFERENCES: *There exists a strong ordering S such that, for each i, $x\,R_i\,y$ and $B(x, y, z)$ together imply $y\,P_i\,z$, where $B(x, y, z)$ is the betweenness relation derived from S by Definition 12.*

Consideration of a one-peaked graph will show that the above statement corresponds precisely to that given originally.

In the terminology of the present study, Black proposes replacing Condition 1 by

CONDITION 1″: *For all sets of individual orderings $R_1, \cdots, R_n$ satisfying the Assumption of Single-Peaked Preferences, the corresponding social ordering R shall be a weak ordering.*

We have already noted (Theorem 1) that the method of majority decision is a social welfare function satisfying Conditions 1–5 when there are only two alternatives altogether, but that method does not satisfy Condition 1 when there are more than two alternatives. The method of majority decision does, however, satisfy Conditions 2–5 for any number of alternatives. We will show that this method satisfies Condition 1″ and hence is a valid social welfare function for single-peaked preferences.

As before, let $N(x, y)$ be the number of individuals for whom $x R_i y$. Then, by Definition 9, if R is formed by the method of majority decision,

(1) $x R y$ if and only if $N(x, y) \geq N(y, x)$.

LEMMA 6: *If R is formed by the method of majority decision from a given set of individual orderings $R_1, \cdots, R_n$, and if, for all i, $x R_i y$ implies $z P_i w$ (for a given x, y, z, and w), then $x R y$ implies $z R w$.*

PROOF: Suppose the hypothesis holds, and also $x R y$. We wish to prove that $z R w$. By hypothesis, for every individual for whom $x R_i y$, we can also say $z R_i w$, so that

(2) $N(z, w) \geq N(x, y)$.

Also, since $x R y$, we have, by (1),

(3) $N(x, y) \geq N(y, x)$.

If $w R_i z$, then not $z P_i w$. Hence, by hypothesis, not $x R_i y$, and therefore $y R_i x$. That is, $w R_i z$ implies $y R_i x$, so that

(4) $N(y, x) \geq N(w, z)$.

By (2)–(4), $N(z, w) \geq N(w, z)$, so that, by (1), $z R w$.   Q.E.D.

THEOREM 4 (Possibility Theorem for Single-Peaked Preferences): *The method of majority decision is a social welfare function satisfying Condition 1″ and Conditions 2–5 for any number of alternatives, provided the number of individuals is odd.*

PROOF: By Lemma 3, the method of majority decision satisfies Conditions 2–5. Hence, it is only necessary to prove that if $R_1, \cdots, R_n$ satisfy the Assumption of Single-Peaked Preferences, then the social ordering R formed by the method of majority decision satisfies Axioms I and II. Clearly, either $N(x, y) \geq N(y, x)$ or $N(y, x) \geq N(x, y)$, so that, by (1), for all x and y, either $x R y$ or $y R x$. Hence, R satisfies Axiom I.

To show that R is transitive, assume $x R y$ and $y R z$. We seek to prove that $x R z$. If $x = y$, then $x R z$ follows from $y R z$; if $y = z$, then $x R z$ follows from $x R y$. If $x = z$, then we seek to prove that $x R x$; but this follows immediately from (1) and the trivial fact that $N(x, x) \geq N(x, x)$.

Now assume that x, y, and z are distinct. By Lemma 5, there are three possibilities:

(a) $B(x, y, z)$: By the Assumption, if $x R_i y$ holds, then $y P_i z$ holds. From $x R_i y$ and $y P_i z$, it follows that $x P_i z$; i.e., $x R_i y$ implies $x P_i z$.

Now apply Lemma 6, replacing z by x and w by z; from $x \, R \, y$, which is assumed, follows $x \, R \, z$.

(b) $B(y, x, z)$: Suppose $y \, R_i \, z$ but not $x \, P_i \, z$. From the second statement follows $z \, R_i \, x$. From $y \, R_i \, z$ and $z \, R_i \, x$, we can conclude $y \, R_i \, x$. By the Assumption, replacing x by y and y by x, $y \, R_i \, x$ implies $x \, P_i \, z$, which contradicts the original supposition that both $y \, R_i \, z$ and not $x \, P_i \, z$ hold. Therefore, if $y \, R_i \, z$, then $x \, P_i \, z$. By Lemma 6, replacing x by y, y by z, z by x, and w by z, $x \, R \, z$ follows from $y \, R \, z$.

(c) $B(y, z, x)$: Suppose $y \, R_i \, z$. Then, by the Assumption, replacing x by y, y by z, and z by x, we can assert $z \, P_i \, x$. From $y \, R_i \, z$ and $z \, P_i \, x$, we have $y \, P_i \, x$. That is,

(5) $$y \, R_i \, z \text{ implies } y \, P_i \, x.$$

Let N' be the number of individuals for whom $y \, P_i \, x$, and N the number of individuals. Then, $x \, R_i \, y$ if and only if not $y \, P_i \, x$, so that

(6) $$N(x, y) = N - N'.$$

If $y \, P_i \, x$, then certainly $y \, R_i \, x$, so that

(7) $$N(y, x) \geq N'.$$

Since $x \, R \, y$, we have, by (1), that $N(x, y) \geq N(y, x)$; by (6) and (7), $N - N' \geq N'$, or

(8) $$N' \leq \frac{N}{2}.$$

From (5),

(9) $$N' \geq N(y, z).$$

For each i, either $y \, R_i \, z$ or $z \, R_i \, y$; therefore,

(10) $$N(y, z) + N(z, y) \geq N.$$

As $y \, R \, z$, we have, by (1), that $N(y, z) \geq N(z, y)$. By (10), this implies that $N(y, z) \geq N/2$. From (9), it follows that $N' \geq N/2$, and, with the aid of (8), $N' = N/2$. But this contradicts the hypothesis that the number of voters is odd. Hence, case (c) cannot arise; if $B(y, z, x)$, then we cannot have both $x \, R \, y$ and $y \, R \, z$.

Therefore, in every case where it was possible that $x \, R \, y$ and $y \, R \, z$, it was also true that $x \, R \, z$. R is transitive; this completes the proof of Theorem 4.

It may be noted that Theorem 1, the Possibility Theorem for Two Alternatives, is really a special case of Theorem 4 since, if there are only two alternatives, the individual orderings are necessarily single-peaked. The case of complete unanimity, discussed in the last section, is also a case of single-peaked preferences if alternatives that are indifferent to every individual are regarded as identical, for we may then use as the basic strong ordering the common individual ordering. Also note that in the example of the paradox of voting mentioned in Chapter I, Section 1, there was no way of ordering the three alternatives so that the orderings were of the single-peaked variety.

The condition in Theorem 4 that the number of individuals be odd is essential. Suppose there are two individuals, one of whom prefers x to y and y to z, while the other prefers y to z and z to x. These orderings satisfy the Assumption of Single-Peaked Preferences if the ordering x, y, z is taken as the basic strong ordering. Then majority decision yields x indifferent to y and y preferred to z, but x is indifferent and not preferred to z.

Thus, if the Assumption of Single-Peaked Preferences is satisfied by the orderings of the various individuals, assumed odd in number, we could, under certain assumptions about the environment, find the social choice by considering each pair of alternatives, having individuals vote between them, and then selecting that alternative which has a majority over every other in pair-wise comparisons. Actually, as Black points out, if the Assumption is made, it is not necessary to make all those comparisons to find the optimum; it suffices to look only at the first choices of the various individuals and find the median of these first choices when they are considered arrayed according to the basic strong ordering.[7]

The fact that Black's restrictions on individual orderings suffice to permit a social welfare function casts new light on what is meant by similarity of social attitudes. In the present case, individuals can have varied first choices; but they must have a fundamentally similar attitude toward the classification of the alternatives since they all order the alternatives in the same way.[8]

[7] Black, "Decisions of a Committee . . . ," *op. cit.*, p. 250.

[8] I may add here that Black intended his work to be a contribution to the analysis of actual political behavior rather than to that of social welfare. He envisages a committee before which successive motions come. The committee chooses between the first two motions; then the winning motion is paired off against the third for voting; and, similarly, the motion which has emerged victorious after the first n votes is now voted on with the $(n + 1)$th motion as the alternative. However, Black assumes that, at each stage in the process, each individual votes in accordance with his ordering. This could only be so if no individual had any incentive to misrepresent his true feelings in order to get a final result more to his liking; if this were so, then certainly no individual would misrepresent his ordering if he knew that nobody else would. An example will show the last statement to be false. Let individual 1 have ordering x, y, z; individual 2, y, x, z; and individual 3, z, y, x. Suppose that the motions come up in the order y, z, x. If all individuals voted according to their

3. THE IDEALIST POSITION AND THE CONCEPT OF CONSENSUS

The results of the preceding two sections show that mathematically, at least, it is possible to construct suitable social welfare functions if we feel entitled to say in advance that the tastes of individuals fall within certain prescribed realms of similarity. Do these or possibly other mathematical restrictions have any social significance? I do not pretend to have any definite answer; but some reflections and tentative suggestions are in order, especially on the relation between the mathematics and the views contained in a small sample of the vast literature on the foundations of social morality.

The assumption of Section 1, that of complete agreement among individuals on the ordering of social alternatives, may seem obviously contrary to fact. But, properly interpreted, it is at the basis of a great portion of political philosophy, namely, the idealist school. The fundamental doctrine of the group is that we must distinguish between the individual will, as it exists at any given instant under varying external influences, and the general will, which is supposed to inhere in all and which is the same in all; social morality is based on the latter. This view is expressed in the works of Rousseau, Kant, and T. H. Green, among many others.[9] There may, indeed, be wide divergencies between

---

orderings, y would be chosen over z and then over x. However, individual 1 could vote for z the first time, insuring its victory; then, in the choice between z and x, x would win if individuals 2 and 3 voted according to their orderings, so that individual 1 would have a definite incentive to misrepresent. The problem treated here is similar to, though not identical with, the majority game, and the complicated analysis needed to arrive at rational solutions there suggests strongly the difficulties of this more general problem of voting. (See von Neumann and Morgenstern, *op. cit.*, pp. 431–445.) This difficulty is noted by Black ("On the Rationale . . . ," *op. cit.*, p. 29 fn.).

[9] J. J. Rousseau, *The Social Contract*, English translation, New York and London: G. P. Putnam's Sons, second edition, revised, 1906, p. 25; I. Kant, "Fundamental Principles of the Metaphysic of Morals," in *Kant's Critique of Practical Reason and Other Works on the Theory of Ethics*, English translation by T. K. Abbott, fifth edition, New York: Longmans, Green and Co., 1898, pp. 51–52; T. H. Green, *Lectures on the Principles of Political Obligation*, New York and London: Longmans, Green and Co., 1895, pp. 44–48, 125–126. "To [a basis of political or free society] it is necessary, not indeed that everyone subject to the laws should take part in voting them, still less that he should consent to their application to himself, but that it should represent an idea of common good, which each member of the society can make his own so far as he is rational, i.e., capable of the conception of a common good, however much particular passions may lead him to ignore it and thus necessitate the use of force to prevent him from doing that which, so far as influenced by the conception of a common good, he would willingly abstain from" (Green, *ibid.*, p. 126). (See also Knight, "Ethics and Economic Reform," *op. cit.*, p. 78.)

the individual will, corrupted by the environment, and the true general will, which can never err though it may be mistaken as to means; indeed, the two wills will only agree by accident.[10] But the existence of the general will as the basis for the very existence of a society is insisted on.[11]

Kant has developed the idealistic viewpoint in morals in the most systematic fashion. He distinguished among three imperatives for an individual: the technical, the pragmatic, and the moral. The technical imperative is identical with what we have here called the environment; it represents knowledge of the means necessary to carry out given ends. The pragmatic imperative is the direction to the individual to seek his happiness; it corresponds to our individual orderings of social alternatives. Happiness is, according to Kant, a vague and uncertain guide to action. These two imperatives are of a contingent nature, lacking in the ultimate necessity which should characterize moral obligation; hence, he refers to them as hypothetical imperatives, as contrasted with the moral imperative, which is a categorical imperative having an objective existence.[12] The moral imperative corresponds to our concept of the social ordering, in a sense, but it is also an individual ordering for every individual; it is the will which every individual would have if he were fully rational.

The content of the moral imperative stems from its categorical nature. The moral or categorical imperative must have full interpersonal validity; this is Kant's principle of the Autonomy of the Will. For this to hold, each individual must treat every other individual as an end in himself. Kant's famous rule of the categorical imperative is, then, to adopt such principles of behavior that, if everyone followed them, they would lead to no self-contradiction. A group of individuals each rationally obeying the moral imperative constitutes a "kingdom of ends"— in our terminology, a society with a satisfactory social welfare function.[13]

The idealist doctrine then may be summed up by saying that each individual has two orderings, one which governs him in his everyday

[10] Rousseau, op. cit., p. 35.

[11] Rousseau: "If the opposition of individual interests has rendered the establishment of societies necessary, it is the accord of these same interests which has rendered it possible" (ibid., p. 34). Green: "There can be no right without a consciousness of common interest on the part of members of a society. Without this there might be certain powers on the part of individuals, but no recognition of these powers by others as powers of which they allow the exercise, nor any claim to such recognition; and without this recognition or claim to recognition there can be no right" (op. cit., p. 48); "No one therefore can have a right except (1) as a member of a society, and (2) of a society in which some common good is recognised as their own ideal good, as that which should be for each of them" (ibid., p. 44).

[12] Kant, op. cit., p. 34.

[13] Ibid., pp. 51–52.

actions and one which would be relevant under some ideal conditions and which is in some sense truer than the first ordering. It is the latter which is considered relevant to social choice, and it is assumed that there is complete unanimity with regard to the truer individual ordering.

It is overly strong to require that the pragmatic imperatives of different individuals be identical and perhaps even too much to ask that there exist moral imperatives which have this property. The results of Section 2 show that the condition of unanimity is mathematically unnecessary to the existence of a social welfare function, and we may well hope that there are still other conditions than those laid down there under which the formation of social welfare functions, possibly other than the method of majority decision, will be possible. But it must be demanded that there be some sort of consensus on the ends of society, or no social welfare function can be formed. If we deny the possibility or meaningfulness of two wills, the consensus must be found in the overtly expressed individual orderings; if we accept the possibility, we may find the desired agreement in the moral imperatives of the various members of society.

The importance of consensus on ends as part of the process of making judgments on matters of social welfare has been stressed by economists of both the Left and Right persuasions. Professor Knight is very explicit. "We contend not only that such ideals are real to individuals, but that they are part of our culture and sufficiently uniform and objective to form a useful standard of comparison for a given country at a given time." [14] This formulation is especially valuable for pointing out that the consensus of moral imperatives need not be grounded in a metaphysical absolute but may be based on the relative socio-ethical norms of a particular culture. Implicit in Knight's stand is the inference that there are two wills; as noted below, he evidently regards the moral imperative as having to be discovered by special techniques, which would hardly be the case if the concept of consensus applied to the pragmatic imperatives of individuals.

Professor Stigler has made it a burden of reproach to the new welfare economics that it does not take into account the consensus on ends.[15] It is not clear from his discussion whether he regards the agreed-on ends as being obvious from introspection or casual observation (i.e., relating to the pragmatic imperatives) or as requiring special inquiry; his comments seem rather to incline in the former direction, in which case he

[14] Knight, "The Ethics of Competition," in *The Ethics of Competition and Other Essays, op. cit.*, pp. 41–45.

[15] G. J. Stigler, "The New Welfare Economics," *American Economic Review*, Vol. 33, June, 1943, pp. 355–359, especially pp. 357–359.

lays himself open to Professor Samuelson's request for immediate enlightenment on various specific economic issues.[16]

The distinction between moral and pragmatic imperatives was one of the strands in the debate a few years back between Mr. Dobb and Professor Lerner.[17] One of Dobb's chief points in denying the possibility of operating a socialist economy under the price system was an attack on the "sacredness of consumers' preferences," especially in the matter of time-preference. "In judgment of the future, the 'natural' individual is notoriously unreliable."[18] In this question and in such matters as the number of varieties of goods to be put on the market, it is held that collective choices are superior to individual ones; his reference to a Gresham's law of tastes is a clear indication of the distinction between moral and pragmatic imperatives and the need for special methods of choice to arrive at the imperative. The liability of the individual will to corruption enters in Dobb's emphasis on the variability of individual tastes in the presence of advertising and of the emergence of new products.[19] His remarks are not too far from Kant's about the vagueness and uncertainty of the drive for personal happiness as a guide to action. Lerner quite justly observes that Dobb "implies some transcendental optimum other than that shown 'by a free market or in any other way' ";[20] and Dobb himself, with the rationalistic tradition common to utilitarianism and Marxism in his mind, grows a little worried: "Yet I do not wish to follow Kant and 'limit knowledge in order to make way for faith.' Planned economy will have its economic laws," though he does not specify them.[21]

Dobb's work presents clearly the dilemma posed by accepting the doctrine of consensus as a foundation for social ethics. Empirically, we can reject the idea that the consensus can be found in the expressed individual wills. If consensus is to be found in the moral imperative, what is the basis for it? Ethical absolutism is unsatisfying to a mind brought up in the liberal heritage, however much specific shortcomings

[16] P. A. Samuelson, "Further Comment on Welfare Economics," *American Economic Review*, Vol. 33, September, 1943, p. 605 fn.

[17] M. H. Dobb, "Economic Theory and the Problems of a Socialist Economy," *Economic Journal*, Vol. 43, December, 1933, pp. 588–598; A. P. Lerner, "Economic Theory and Socialist Economy," *Review of Economic Studies*, Vol. 2, October, 1934, pp. 51–61; M. H. Dobb, "A Reply," *ibid.*, February, pp. 144–151; A. P. Lerner, "A Rejoinder," *ibid.*, pp. 152–154.

[18] Dobb, "Economic Theory and the Problems of a Socialist Economy," *op. cit.*, pp. 591–593.

[19] Dobb, "A Reply," *op. cit.*, pp. 147–148.

[20] Lerner, "Economic Theory and Socialist Economy," *ibid.*, p. 58.

[21] Dobb, "Economic Theory and the Problems of a Socialist Economy," *op. cit.*, p. 597.

in the liberal formulation are rejected. Knight's version, depending on ethical relativism, leads to the danger of a glorification of the status quo, though it still seems to be the better alternative.

From the point of view of seeking a consensus of the moral imperative of individuals, such consensus being assumed to exist, the problem of choosing an electoral or other choice mechanism, or, more broadly, of choosing a social structure, assumes an entirely different form from that discussed in the greater part of this study. The essential problem becomes that of choosing our mechanism so as best to bring the pragmatic imperative into coincidence with the moral. It is from this point of view that Rousseau discusses the relative merits of different forms of government.[22]

In this aspect, the case for democracy rests on the argument that free discussion and expression of opinion are the most suitable techniques of arriving at the moral imperative implicitly common to all.[23] Voting, from this point of view, is not a device whereby each individual expresses his personal interests, but rather where each individual gives his opinion of the general will.[24]

This model has much in common with the statistical problem of pooling the opinions of a group of experts to arrive at a best judgment; here individuals are considered experts at detecting the moral imperative.[25]

[22] Rousseau, *op. cit.*, Book III, Chapters IV–VII.

[23] "All opinions, yea errors, known, read and collated, are of main service and assistance towards the speedy attainment of what is truest." (John Milton, "Areopagitica," in *Complete Poetry and Selected Prose of John Milton*, New York: Modern Library, 1942, p. 690.)

[24] Rousseau, *op. cit.*, pp. 165–166. "The principle of majority rule must be taken ethically as a means of ascertaining a real 'general will,' not as a mechanism by which one set of interests is made subservient to another set. Political discussion must be assumed to represent a quest for an objectively ideal or 'best' policy, not a contest between interests." (Knight, "Economic Theory and Nationalism," *op. cit.*, p. 296 fn.) The inner quotes point up all the difficulties beautifully. A similar view was expressed by Professor Simons. (See H. C. Simons, "Introduction: A Political Credo," in *Economic Policy for a Free Society*, Chicago: The University of Chicago Press, 1948, pp. 7–9.)

[25] This analogy was pointed out to me by O. Helmer. The problem in question is an application of R. A. Fisher's discriminant analysis. An interesting contribution is that of G. L. Schuyler ("The Ordering of n Items Assigned to k Rank Categories by Votes of m Individuals," *Journal of the American Statistical Association*, Vol. 43, December, 1948, pp. 559–563). Schuyler's suggestion is essentially a rank-order method of voting, modified by weighting the various individuals in such a way as to make them more comparable. Considered simply as a device for reconciling opposing interests, it would fall under the ban of Theorem 2; however, it is regarded rather as a method of reconciling different estimates of some objective reality. The probability implications of the model are not worked out, and the most interesting question for political theory, the weighting of the individuals in terms of their intrinsic ability to judge, is blinked.

An antidemocrat might argue that only a minority are sufficiently capable of discerning the moral imperative beneath the obscuring veil of the pragmatic to make them useful experts in this sense; thus Plato calls for a small specialized group of guardians to make the social choices. A prodemocrat might argue that all men have natively an equal portion of the light; all are children of God. The analogy to the problem of pooling experts' opinions is, of course, incomplete; for, in the social welfare problem, the very method of pooling, i.e., of social decision, may affect the degree of expertness of individuals. For example, marking off a certain group, such as army officers, to hold power may, because of the greater leisure and better living conditions which follow, enable them to make better decisions, even though there is no native superiority to the remainder of the society; or it may cause them to lose contact with the daily problems of the ordinary man and so lower their ability to make "good" decisions in certain contexts. More broadly, the very act of establishing a dictator or elite to decide on the social good may lead to a distortion of the pragmatic from the moral imperative. "Power always corrupts; and absolute power corrupts absolutely" (Lord Acton).

Any view which depends on consensus as the basis for social action certainly implies that the market mechanism cannot be taken as the social welfare function since that mechanism cannot take account of the altruistic motives which must be present to secure that consensus. If, in particular, the consensus in question is that of moral imperatives, the case is even worse since the market can certainly only express pragmatic imperatives. This does not deny the possibility of a limited use of the market as an instrument for achieving certain parts of the social optimum, especially if it is deliberately manipulated to make behavior under pragmatic imperatives coincide with that which would exist under moral ones.

4. Knowledge and the Meaning of Social Alternatives

The distinction between the overtly expressed will and some truer desires may be put in a slightly different way. Any individual may be presumed to have some ultimate values, partly biological, partly specific to the culture pattern; these are, however, largely unconscious. His overt preferences are for values instrumental in achieving these ultimate values. The relation between the two sets of values is not unique; for a given set of ultimate values, there may be differing sets of instrumental values, depending on the greater or lesser knowledge of the individual as to the best means of achieving his ultimate values and as to what his ultimate values are. The second type of ignorance seems to be particularly in the mind of Dobb, for example, as discussed in the last section, and all through the idealist tradition. The reality of the first type of ignorance in economic life is well evidenced by the fact that the price ratio between two chemically indistinguishable brands of aspirin has exceeded ten to one; here the hierarchy of instrumental values leads to different preferences for different brands of aspirin, though they are in fact equally efficacious in achieving the ultimate end of mitigating headaches. Though welfare economics in its formal aspects typically takes individuals' overt behavior as unanalyzable, few economists would oppose laws against false advertising.

In this connection, it must be pointed out that the *alternatives*, among which social preference is to be defined, may be interpreted in (at least) two ways: (1) each alternative is a vector whose components are values of the various particular decisions actually made by the government, such as tax rates, expenditures, antimonopoly policy, and price policies of socialized enterprise; (2) each alternative is a complete description of the state of every individual throughout the future. For convenience, we shall refer to the first interpretation of the concept "alternative" as the concept "social decision," to the second as the concept "social end." Social ends either are themselves ultimate ends or at least completely determine the ultimate ends; the relation between social ends and ultimate ends is unknown only to the extent that the ultimate ends are unknown. On the other hand, it is also true that social decisions determine, wholly or partially, social ends; but the relation here is a matter, in part, of the empirical laws of the social sciences. In the present state of these disciplines, it is too much to expect the relations to be well known. Therefore, the relation between the orderings concerning social ends and those concerning social decisions is afflicted with uncertainty.

One of the great advantages of abstract postulational methods is the fact that the same system may be given several different interpretations, permitting a considerable saving of time. In the present case, the argument given in Chapter V is valid whether the variables, x, y, $\cdots$, are assumed to refer to social decisions or social ends. It might therefore be argued that the problem is equally acute in either case. However, it could be held that, since ultimate ends arise out of biological and cultural needs, they are, in part at least, objective. Thus, orderings of social ends, while not identical from individual to individual, are likely to be more similar than individual preference scales for social decisions. It may be that the biological and cultural basis of ultimate ends limits preferences about them sufficiently so that a social welfare function can be formed; then the social ordering of social decisions should be based on the social ordering of social ends plus the use of scientific and statistical methods to limit the amount of ignorance in passing from decisions to ends and to limit the effects of the remaining ignorance.

It may also be remarked that, in terms of the analysis in the present section, the doctrine of "enlightened self-interest" would be justified in the event that it is assumed that all individuals have the same ultimate ends for the community. In that case, different opinions on social issues arise from lack of knowledge and can be removed by discovering the truth and letting it be widely known. In our present pessimistic age, even this seems like a very difficult problem, not to be dismissed as lightly as it was by our more exuberant predecessors of the last century.

The fact of uncertainty as to the relation between decisions and ends has important implications for the controversy as to the relative efficiency of centralized and decentralized planning, particularly in a dynamic economy. It may well be argued that centralized planning will necessarily reduce this uncertainty since more facts are available to the central planners.[26] It is true that the effect of a given error may be greater under centralization; but this will not be so if a rational method of planning against uncertainty is adopted.[27] The relation of uncertainty to the optimum form of the economic system has been insufficiently explored in the recent formal work on welfare economics,[28] probably because of the lack of a well-developed theory of behavior under uncertainty. Thus, the stimulating discussion of Professor Hicks [29] is vitiated by his very restricted certainty-equivalent theory of uncertainty, the limitations of which have been very well shown by Professors Hart and Friedman.[30]

[26] This point has been stressed by Dobb, especially in relation to investment decisions and the possibility of obsolescence. ("Economic Theory and the Problems of a Socialist Economy," *op. cit.*, pp. 596–597; also "A Note on Saving and Investment in a Socialist Economy," *Economic Journal*, Vol. 49, December, 1939, pp. 726–727.)

[27] The type of flexibility required for rational planning against uncertainty has been well described by A. G. Hart ("Risk, Uncertainty, and the Unprofitability of Compounding Probabilities," in *Studies in Mathematical Economics and Econometrics*, O. Lange, F. McIntyre, and T. O. Yntema, eds., Chicago: The University of Chicago Press, 1942, pp. 110–118). The rational theory of planning against uncertainty is identical with the foundations of statistical inference (see A. Wald, "Foundations of a General Theory of Sequential Decision Functions," *Econometrica*, Vol. 15, October, 1947, pp. 279–313).

[28] The most systematic discussion is that of Reder, *op. cit.*, Chapter VII.

[29] J. R. Hicks, *Value and Capital*, second edition, Oxford: The Clarendon Press, 1946, p. 135.

[30] Hart, *op. cit.;* M. Friedman, "Lange on Price Flexibility and Employment: A Methodological Criticism," *American Economic Review*, Vol. 36, September, 1946, pp. 627–630.

5. PARTIAL UNANIMITY

The discussion of the last two sections suggests, however vaguely, that the solution of the social welfare problem may lie in some generalization of the unanimity condition of Section 1, applied perhaps to individual orderings found by special inquiries rather than those overtly expressed. But the correct mathematical generalization of the unanimity condition is not easy to see. Black's postulate, elegant though it be, is not obviously applicable, though perhaps deeper investigation would change the verdict.

An attempted generalization which immediately suggests itself is to assume that all individuals are unanimous about some choices but not necessarily about others. That is, among all possible ordered pairs (x, y) of social alternatives, there are some for which it is known that all individuals feel alike. These common feelings can be expressed by saying that there is a quasi-ordering Q of all social alternatives such that the orderings of all individuals are compatible with this same quasi-ordering. If there are three alternatives such that Q tells us nothing about the comparison of any two, i.e., if there are three alternatives such that we do not assume unanimity of agreement as to the choice between any two, then clearly the assumption of a partial unanimity does not exclude any of the three alternatives in question.

This result can be rigorously deduced from Theorem 3. First, suppose that not merely is it known that certain choices will be unanimous but in fact it is known in advance what the choice will be. That is, suppose Q is known in advance. If we let S be the set of three alternatives mentioned above, then Theorem 3 applies with $Q_1, \cdots, Q_n$, all Q's being the same. If now we merely postulate unanimity of those choices without specifying how the choices will come out, we have clearly imposed less restraint on the orderings of individuals, and therefore a fortiori it remains valid that the only possible social welfare functions are imposed or dictatorial.

6. THE DECISION PROCESS AS A VALUE

Up to now, no attempt has been made to find guidance by considering the components of the vector which defines the social state. One especially interesting analysis of this sort considers that, among the variables which taken together define the social state, one is the very process by which the society makes its choice. This is especially important if the mechanism of choice itself has a value to the individuals in the society.

For example, an individual may have a positive preference for achieving a given distribution through the free market mechanism over achieving the same distribution through rationing by the government. If the decision process is interpreted broadly to include the whole socio-psychological climate in which social decisions are made, the reality and importance of such preferences, as opposed to preferences about the distributions of goods, are obvious.

From a logical point of view, some care has to be taken in defining the decision process since the choice of decision process in any given case is made by a decision process. There is no deep circularity here, however. If x is the vector describing a possible social state, let x_1 be the components of that vector which are not decision processes; let x_2 be the process of deciding among the alternative possible x_1's; in general, let x_n be the process of deciding among the alternative possible x_{n-1}'s. We may refer to x_1 as the first-order decision, x_2 as a second-order decision, etc.; then an nth-order decision is a process of choosing an $(n-1)$th-order decision method. Any particular social state is described in its entirety by a vector of the form $(x_1, x_2, \cdots, x_n, \cdots)$. In describing the United States Government, we might say that x_1 is a proposed bill or, more precisely, the proposed bill taken into conjunction with all the legislation now on the books; x_2 is the process by which bills are enacted into law by Congress and the President; x_3 is the process of choosing a Congress and President, set down by the Constitution; and x_4 is the process of constitutional amendment.

Suppose that for some value of n there is one possible x_n which is so strongly desired by all individuals that they prefer any social state which involves accepting that particular x_n to any which does not.[31] For example, the belief in democracy may be so strong that any decision on the distribution of goods arrived at democratically may be preferred to such a decision arrived at in other ways, even though all individuals might have preferred the second distribution of goods to the first if it had been arrived at democratically. Similarly, the desire for a dictator-ship or for a particular dictator may be overwhelming under certain conditions. In such a case, again, our social welfare problem may be regarded as solved since the unanimous agreement on the decision process may resolve the conflicts as to the decisions themselves.

Some such valuation as the above seems to be implicit in every stable political structure. However, there is a certain empirical element in practice; individuals prefer certain political structures over others, not only because of their liking for the structure as such, but also because

---

[31] Cf. Rousseau, *op. cit.*, pp. 18–19: "The law of plurality of votes is itself estab-lished by agreement, and supposes unanimity at least in the beginning."

they have some idea of the preference patterns of the other individuals in the society and feel that on the whole they can expect the particular structure in question, taken in conjunction with the expected behavior of other individuals under that structure, to yield decisions on current matters which will usually be acceptable to themselves.   Thus, we may expect that social welfare judgments can usually be made when there is both a widespread agreement on the decision process and a widespread agreement on the desirability of everyday decisions.   Indeed, the sufficiency of the former alone, as implied in the preceding paragraph, would require that individuals ascribe an incommensurably greater value to the process than to the decisions reached under it, a proposition which hardly seems like a credible representation of the psychology of most individuals in a social situation.

Chapter VIII

NOTES ON THE THEORY OF SOCIAL CHOICE, 1963

When the first edition of this book was prepared, the relevant literature was summarized in four pages. Since 1951 there has been a considerably greater volume of discussion. In preparing a second edition, I felt that the most useful procedure would be to append to my previous discussion a series of reflections inspired by the recent discussions. Despite their high quality, I do not find it obligatory to prepare a revision of the text itself. It is not the results that have been significantly affected [1] but their interpretation and the relation to other contemporary work. There is no attempt here at exhausting the relevant references.

Let me begin by calling attention to some excellent expositions of the theory of social choice which have appeared in the last decade. A remarkably clear exposition at an elementary level has been given by M. Barbut.[2] A number of interesting papers on the foundations of welfare economics has appeared in a special issue of *Économie Appliquée*.[3] I particularly call attention to a remarkable exposition of the theory of collective choice and the general problem of aggregation due to G.-Th. Guilbaud.[4]

A recent paper by W. Vickrey [5] has reviewed the proof of the main theorem of this book under somewhat different assumptions and traced out some possible implications and further lines of development in the foundations of the theory. By restating the axioms in a somewhat different form, he has achieved an extremely simple exposition which brings out the lines of the argument very clearly.

Perhaps the most complete and up-to-date summary of the problem of

[1] There are, however, some revisions that must be made in precise mathematical statements, as Blau (see Section II.4) has shown.

[2] "Quelques aspects mathématiques de la décision rationnelle," *Les Temps Modernes*, Vol. 15, October, 1959, pp. 725–45, trans. as "Does the Majority Ever Rule?" *Portfolio and Art News Annual*, No. 4, 1961, pp. 79–83, 161–68.

[3] Volume 5, October–December, 1952.

[4] "Les théories de l'intérêt général et la problème logique de l'agrégation," *ibid.*, pp. 501–84.

[5] "Utility, Strategy, and Social Decision Rules," *Quarterly Journal of Economics*, Vol. 74, November, 1960, pp. 507–35.

aggregation of individual choices into collective ones, with particular emphasis on political aspects, has been carried out by W. Riker.[6] The economic literature has been ably reviewed by J. Rothenberg.[7]

Finally, it should be noted that the pioneer work of D. Black (see pp. 75–80 of the text) has recently been collected and systematically expounded in a book.[8]

I. Historical Remarks

I must confess to a certain want of diligence in tracking down the historical origins of the theories of social choice. When I first studied the problem and developed the contradictions in the majority rule system, I was sure that this was no original discovery, although I had no explicit reference, and sought to express this knowledge by referring to the "well-known 'paradox of voting' " (text, p. 2). When the basic ideas of the book were first read as a paper to the Econometric Society in December, 1948, Professor C. P. Wright of the University of New Brunswick called my attention to the work of E. J. Nanson.[9] Nanson, in discussing a proposal of his for a method of election, refers without great emphasis to the possibility of intransitivity arising from majority choice (pp. 213–214) for which he gives no previous reference. It is true, however, that the tone of his remarks does not suggest that this possibility is a discovery of his own, although it is rather difficult to be sure.

However, Guilbaud [10] notes that the paradox was known and developed by the Marquis de Condorcet in the eighteenth century,[11] and refers to the paradox therefore as the Condorcet effect. This development was part of Condorcet's great interest in methods of election and essentially, therefore, in the theory of social choice. His work, in turn,

[6] "Voting and the Summation of Preferences: An Interpretive Bibliographic Review of Selected Developments During the Last Decade," *American Political Science Review*, Vol. 55, December, 1961, pp. 900–11.

[7] J. Rothenberg, *The Measurement of Social Welfare*, Englewood Cliffs, New Jersey: Prentice-Hall, 1961.

[8] *The Theory of Committees and Elections*, Cambridge, U. K.: Cambridge University Press, 1958.

[9] "Methods of Election," *Transactions and Proceedings of the Royal Society of Victoria*, Vol. 19, 1882, pp. 197–240.

[10] *Op. cit.*, pp. 513–15.

[11] Most especially in his *Essai sur l'application de l'analyse à la probabilité des décisions rendues à la pluralité des voix*, Paris, 1785. A thorough study of Condorcet's thought appears in G.-G. Granger, *La Mathématique Social du Marquis de Condorcet*, Paris: Presses Universitaires de France, 1956. The work of Condorcet on voting is mostly analyzed in Chapter 3, especially pp. 94–129, an extensive summary of Condorcet's *Essai*.

seems to have been inspired by an earlier paper, that of Jean-Charles de Borda.[12]

Black [13] has given a history of the theory of social choice, starting with the work of Borda and including that of Condorcet, Laplace, Nanson, Galton, and most especially C. L. Dodgson (Lewis Carroll). In regard to the last, he has uncovered some previously unpublished pamphlets in which Dodgson cryptically, although with great acumen, analyzed problems of elections and particularly what he called "cyclical majorities." Both Dodgson's work and Black's comments on it and on the circumstances of its origin are extremely worthwhile.

Black's excellent history makes superfluous any need for recapitulation here. However, there are a few comments that may be of some interest. Borda's starting point is the fact that plurality voting among several candidates could easily lead to a very unreasonable choice. His major point—and this, I believe, has been decisive in all subsequent work—is that the entire ordering of the individual voters among alternative candidates is needed for social decision. The method Borda proposes is the rank-order method as defined on p. 27 of the present text. This, as Borda observes, gives equal weight to the differences between adjacent candidates as well as to different voters. The first raises thus the problem of the measurability of utility, the second that of interpersonal comparisons. He justifies the first step by an argument essentially based on ignorance. If a voter ranks B between A and C, then we have as much reason to suppose that the difference in intensity between A and B is greater than the difference in intensity between B and C as to suppose that it is less. The adding up of different individual votes is justified on the grounds of equality of voters. These themes have continued to recur. The argument of L. Goodman and H. Markowitz [14] may be regarded as giving in effect an axiomatic justification of Borda's position.

As Granger and Black both observed, Condorcet has really two different approaches. In the one most in line with subsequent developments, as well as with Borda's work, the chief contribution has been what might be termed the *Condorcet criterion*, that a candidate who receives a majority as against each other candidate should be elected.

---

[12] "Mémoire sur les élections au scrutin," *Mémoires de l'Académie Royale des Sciences*, 1781, pp. 657–65. The paper was presented in 1770. For an English translation and incisive comments, see A. de Grazia, "Mathematical Derivation of an Election System," *Isis*, Vol. 44, June, 1953, pp. 42–51.

[13] *Op. cit.* in footnote 8, Part II.

[14] "Social Welfare Functions Based on Individual Rankings," *American Journal of Sociology*, Vol. 58, November, 1952, pp. 257–62.

This implicitly accepts the view of what I have termed the independence of irrelevant alternatives (see text, pp. 26–28). It was in this context that Condorcet discovered that pairwise majority comparisons might lead to intransitivity and hence to an indeterminacy in the social choice. Condorcet did propose some methods for dealing with the general case, but these have not been found clear by subsequent writers.

The second approach is closely related to the theory of juries which Condorcet and others were studying. Here the implication is rather that the voters are judges of some truth rather than expressing their own preferences. This position is essentially a stochastic version of an idealistic position and has been discussed previously (see text, pp. 85–86).

The work of Nanson and Dodgson deserves some mention, although we must refer to Black's work and the original sources for fuller treatment. Both criticize various well-known methods of voting, mainly in terms of failing to satisfy the Condorcet criterion. Most proposed methods do not even accomplish this much, not even the rank-order method of Borda. Nanson suggests the following procedure based on having the orderings of every voter for all candidates: Rank the candidates according to the rank-order method. Then eliminate all those whose total votes is less than the average. With the remaining candidates form the rank-orders again, considering only those candidates, and repeat the process until one candidate is selected. Nanson shows that if there exists a candidate who has a majority against any other, he will be selected. Of course, the paradox of voting cannot be eliminated by this technique.

Dodgson accepts fully the Condorcet criterion, so much so that he comes to the conclusion that if a cyclical majority persists, then there should be "no election." [15] This position is rather curious. Indeed, Dodgson elsewhere shrewdly points out that "no election," if it is an allowable alternative, should be considered on a par with all the candidates.[16] This seems quite inconsistent with the previous statement. It does point, however, to an important empirical truth, especially about legislative matters rather than the choice of candidates: The status quo does have a built-in edge over all alternative proposals.

Rather interestingly, though, in a discussion of alternative proposals for the case of cyclical majorities,[17] he points out the unreasonableness of their conclusions by reference to another criterion; namely, he points out that the candidate who would have a majority over all others with the least number of interchanges of orderings on the individual prefer-

---

[15] Black, op. cit., p. 230.
[16] Black, op. cit., p. 232.
[17] Black, op. cit., pp. 227–30.

ence scales is not chosen. This suggests that one could elevate this to a principle for election when we do not admit the possibility of "no election," or do not wish to give that alternative any preference. In principle, and especially with computing machines, the criterion itself provides a method of choosing candidates. I do not know whether there is any simple way of characterizing this principle. It does coincide with Nanson's method for the case of three candidates.

II. The Formal Statement of the Conditions and a New Exposition of the Proof

This section consists of some diverse observations on the formal aspects of the theory. First, I show that some of the conditions can be replaced by the Pareto principle (that a unanimity of individual preferences implies a social preference). Since the Pareto principle is universally accepted, the new set of conditions will be easier to compare with other formulations of the problem of social choice. Second, I give what appears to be the simplest formulation of the proof that the conditions are inconsistent. Third, I state some other, stronger, conditions leading to majority rule of some type; these developments are due to May and Murakami. Finally, I comment on an error in the original statement of the theorem, which was discovered by Blau.

1. The Pareto Principle and the Conditions for a Social Welfare Function

The Pareto principle was originally given in the text (p. 36) as a form of the compensation principle. We give it here in a slightly weaker form (involving only strict preferences).

CONDITION P: *If $x\ P_i y$ for all i, then $x\ P\ y$.*

(In words, if every individual prefers x to y, then so does society.)

To meet an important objection raised by Blau,[18] which will be discussed in paragraph 4, I will also at this stage replace Conditions 1 and 2 by the stronger

CONDITION 1': *All logically possible orderings of the alternative social states are admissible.*

CONDITION 2': *For a given pair of alternatives, x and y, let the individual preferences be given.* (By Condition 3, these suffice to determine the

[18] J. H. Blau, "The Existence of Social Welfare Functions," *Econometrica*, Vol. 25, April, 1957, pp. 302-13.

social ordering.) *Suppose that x is then raised in some or all of the individual preferences. Then if x was originally socially preferred to y, it remains socially preferred to y after the change.*

Condition 1′ is unnecessarily strong, but it will be useful in permitting a simpler exposition of the proof. Condition 2′ is equivalent to Condition 2 in the presence of Conditions 1′ and 3.

We note here

THEOREM 1: *Condition P is deducible from Conditions 2′, 3, and 4 (Positive Association of Social and Individual Values, Independence of Irrelevant Alternatives, and Citizens' Sovereignty).*

Indeed, Condition P is identical with Consequence 3 (text, p. 54). Consequence 1 (whose proof involves a fallacy pointed out by Blau) is identical with Condition 2′. A careful reading of the proofs of Consequences 2 and 3 (pp. 52–54) shows then that their proofs depend only on Conditions 2′, 3, and 4.

In the next paragraph, the inconsistency of Conditions 1′, 3, P, and 5 will be shown. Since Condition P follows from Conditions 2′, 3, and 4, the inconsistency of Conditions 1′, 2′, 3, 4, and 5 will follow. However, the new list of conditions will be easier to compare with other formulations of the social choice problem; this comparison is made in Section III.1.[19]

2. *A Proof of the General Possibility Theorem* [20]

In this paragraph, we demonstrate

THEOREM 2: *Conditions 1′, 3, P, and 5 are inconsistent.*[21]

Hence the substitution of the Pareto principle for Conditions 2 and 4 does not affect the inconsistency shown in the text. Furthermore,

---

[19] The foregoing does not mean that Condition 2 or 2′ (Positive Association of Social and Individual Values) can be disregarded in the general development of the theory of social choice. It can be replaced by the Pareto principle for the purpose of demonstrating the inconsistency of the original set of conditions; but if one of the other conditions is dropped in an effort to find a consistent set, then Condition 2 or 2′ is certainly stronger than the Pareto condition (if we continue to maintain Condition 4, the absence of imposed social decisions). For example, a version of Condition 2′ is used by May in constructing a justification for majority rule; see paragraph 3.

[20] This proof originally appeared in my paper, "Le principe de rationalité dans les décisions collectives," *Économie Appliquée*, Vol. 5, October, 1952, pp. 469–84, with, however, some confusing misprints.

[21] Blau states a corresponding theorem (*op. cit.*, p. 309) but adds Condition 2′ to the list of conditions. It appears to be superfluous; the inconsistency holds without assuming Condition 2′ as the subsequent proof will show.

since Condition P follows from Conditions 2, 3, and 4, as shown in the preceding paragraph, this proof also constitutes a proof of the theorem shown in the text (except for the substitution of the stronger Condition 1' for Condition 1). This proof, and indeed any proof of which I am aware, does not differ essentially from that given in the text, but I believe the general lines of the proof and the role played by the different conditions are a little more evident.

We use a slightly different definition of a decisive set than that in the text (Definition 10, p. 52). A set of individuals V is decisive for x against y if x is socially chosen when every individual in V prefers x to y and every individual not in V prefers y to x.

The proof falls into two parts. It is first shown that if an individual is decisive for some pair of alternatives, then he is a dictator, which is excluded by Condition 5; the impossibility theorem itself then follows very easily from the first result and the Pareto principle.

That an individual decisive for some pair of alternatives must be a dictator will be shown to follow from the assumptions of Collective Rationality (Condition 1' together with the definition of a social welfare function), the Pareto principle, and the Independence of Irrelevant Alternatives (Condition 3). We distinguish one individual, called I, and introduce the following notations for statements about the social welfare function, or constitution:

(1) $x \, \overline{D} \, y$ means that x is socially preferred to y whenever I prefers x to y, regardless of the orderings of other individuals;

(2) $x \, D \, y$ means that x is socially preferred to y if individual I prefers x to y and all other individuals have the opposite preference.

This notation is only legitimate because of Condition 3, which assures us that the choice between x and y depends only on the preferences of all individuals concerning those two alternatives. If Condition 2 were assumed, the two concepts would be equivalent (see Consequence 2, p. 53), but we are now assuming the Pareto principle instead.

Note that the statement, $x \, \overline{D} \, y$, implies $x \, D \, y$ and that $x \, D \, y$ is the same as the assertion that I is a decisive set for x against y.

Suppose then that $x \, D \, y$ holds for some x and y. We will first suppose that there are only three alternatives altogether. Let the third alternative be z. Suppose I orders the alternatives, x, y, z, in descending order, whereas all other individuals prefer y to both x and z, but may have any preferences as between the last two. Then I prefers x to y, whereas all others prefer y to x; from (2), this means that $x \, P \, y$. All individuals prefer y to z; by Condition P, $y \, P \, z$. Then by transitivity, $x \, P \, z$; but then this holds whenever $x \, P_I \, z$, regardless of the orderings of other individuals. In symbols,

(3) $$x \, D \, y \text{ implies } x \, \overline{D} \, z.$$

Again suppose $x \, D \, y$, but now suppose that I orders the alternatives, z, x, y, whereas all other individuals prefer both z and y to x. By a similar argument, $x \, P \, y$ and $z \, P \, x$, so that $z \, P \, y$.

(4) $$x \, D \, y \text{ implies } z \, \overline{D} \, y.$$

Interchanging y and z in (4) yields

(5) $$x \, D \, z \text{ implies } y \, \overline{D} \, z.$$

Replacing x by y, y by z, and z by x in (3) yields

(6) $$y \, D \, z \text{ implies } y \, \overline{D} \, x.$$

Since $x \, \overline{D} \, z$ implies $x \, D \, z$, and $y \, \overline{D} \, z$ implies $y \, D \, z$, we can, by chaining the implications (3), (5), and (6), deduce

(7) $$x \, D \, y \text{ implies } y \, \overline{D} \, x.$$

If we interchange x and y in (3), (4), and (7), we arrive at the respective implications

$$y \, D \, x \text{ implies } y \, \overline{D} \, z,$$

$$y \, D \, x \text{ implies } z \, \overline{D} \, x,$$

$$y \, D \, x \text{ implies } x \, \overline{D} \, y,$$

and these can each be chained with the implication (7) to yield

(8) $$x \, D \, y \text{ implies } y \, \overline{D} \, z, z \, \overline{D} \, x, \quad \text{and} \quad x \, \overline{D} \, y.$$

Implications (3), (4), (7), and (8) together can be summarized as saying

(9) *If $x \, D \, y$, then $u \, \overline{D} \, v$ holds for every ordered pair u, v from the three alternatives $x, y,$ and z;*

i.e., individual I is a dictator for the three alternatives.

Because of Condition 1', we can extend this result to any number of alternatives by an argument due to Blau.[22] Suppose $a \, D \, b$ holds, and let x and y be any pair of alternatives. If x and y are the same as a and b, either in the same or in the reverse order, we add a third alternative c to a and b; then we can apply (9) to the triple a, b, c and deduce $x \, \overline{D} \, y$ by letting $u = x, v = y$. If exactly one of x and y is distinct from a and b, add it to a and b to form a triple to which again (9) is applicable. Finally, if both x and y are distinct from a and b, two steps are needed.

[22] *Op. cit.*, p. 310.

First, add x to a and b, and deduce from (9) that $a \, \bar{D} \, x$ and therefore $a \, D \, x$. Then, again applying (9) to the triple a, x, y, we find that $x \, \bar{D} \, y$. Thus, $a \, D \, b$ for some a and b implies that $x \, \bar{D} \, y$ for all x and y, i.e., individual I is a dictator. From the Condition of Nondictatorship (Condition 5), it can be concluded that

(10) $x \, D \, y$ cannot hold for any individual I and any pair x, y.

The remainder of the proof is now an appropriate adaptation of the paradox of voting. By Condition P, there is at least one decisive set for any ordered pair, x, y, namely, the set of all individuals. Among all sets of individuals which are decisive for some pairwise choice, pick one such that no other is smaller; by (10) it must contain at least two individuals. Let V be the chosen set, and let the ordered pair for which it is decisive be x, y. Divide V into two parts, V_1, which contains only a single individual, and V_2, which contains all the rest. Let V_3 be the set of individuals not in V. Consider now the case where the preference order of V_1 is x, y, z, that of all members of V_2 is z, x, y, and that of all members of V_3 is y, z, x.

Since V is decisive for x against y, and all members of V prefer x to y while all others have the opposite preference, $x \, P \, y$. On the other hand, it is impossible that society prefers z to y since that would require that V_2 be decisive on this issue; this is impossible since V_2 has fewer members than V, which, by construction, has as few members as a decisive set can have. Hence, $y \, R \, z$, and, since $x \, P \, y$, society must prefer x to z. But then the single member of V_1 would be decisive, and we have shown that to be impossible.

Thus the contradiction is established.

3. *The Principles of Equality and Neutrality*

Since the conditions given in the text or in the preceding paragraph are inconsistent, there is not much point in strengthening any of them unless another is dropped. One approach most consistent with electoral practice has been to weaken or omit the condition of Collective Rationality. Guilbaud [23] weakens the condition to require simply avoiding contradictions on two successive decisions (rather than three, when the full force of transitivity comes into play). He then conducts the bulk of his analysis under the assumption that the decision rule between any two alternatives be the same. This assumption has later been termed "neutrality," and may be defined formally as follows.

[23] *Op. cit.*, fn. 4, pp. 555–72.

CONDITION OF NEUTRALITY: *Let $T(x)$ be a one-one transformation of the set of alternatives into itself which preserves all individual orderings. Let the environment S be transformed into the environment S' by the transformation T. Then the social choice from S, $C(S)$, is transformed by T into the social choice, $C(S')$, from the environment S'.*

If we confine ourselves to choices among pairs of alternatives, neutrality says essentially that the decisive sets for one pair of alternatives are the same as those for another.

Under the assumption of neutrality, Guilbaud shows that his weaker form of the Collective Rationality condition requires that the decision rules are completely specified by the decisive sets, with the conditions that enlarging a decisive set leads to another decisive set and that the set of all individuals is decisive. Guilbaud then seeks to drop the neutrality assumption and argues that one can extend the previous result by introducing fictitious individuals whose preferences are specified in advance (p. 569). The same results then apply except that the decisive sets may contain these ideal voters.[24]

The principle of neutrality is not intuitively basic, although one expects it to hold in a wide variety of ordinary decisions; practice always insists on special decision rules (special majorities, for example) for particular decisions. K. O. May [25] has combined neutrality with a second and more significant condition.

CONDITION OF EQUALITY: *A permutation of the individual orderings among individuals leaves all social choices unchanged.*

May adds to these conditions a requirement that the social choice be well defined and that a slightly stronger version of the Positive Association of Social and Individual Values holds. For the case of preference (pair-wise choice) which is all that he considers,[26] he shows that major-

[24] The argument is very terse, and I am unable to determine if it is thoroughly correct.

[25] "A Set of Independent Necessary and Sufficient Conditions for Simple Majority Decision," *Econometrica*, Vol. 20, October, 1952, pp. 680–84.

[26] He remarks (*ibid.*, p. 680) that, "Since it follows that the pattern of group choice may be built up if we know the group preferences for each pair of alternatives, the problem [of determining group choices from all sets] reduces to the case of two alternatives." This, however, would only be correct if transitivity were also assumed. Otherwise, there is no necessary connection between choices from two-member sets and choices from larger sets. If there are more than two alternatives, then it is easy to see that many methods of choice satisfy all of May's conditions, for example, both plurality voting and rank-roder summation. A complete characterization of all social decision processes satisfying May's conditions when the number of alternatives is any finite number does not appear to be easy to achieve.

ity voting is the only method of social decision satisfying his conditions.[27]

The Condition of Equality is clearly highly appealing; it is also closely connected with Kant's categorical imperative.

Murakami [28] generalized May's results, making use of some theorems on logical functions. The conditions that social pair-wise choice be well defined and that Condition 2' (see paragraph 1) hold imply that social preference is determined by a generalized form of majority voting. More specifically, there is prescribed a sequence of steps, in each of which decision is made by majority choice, but the outcome of one step may be used as a ballot in the next, and also some ballots with outcomes prescribed in advance may be added to the ballots of real individuals. If, in addition, neutrality is required, then the fixed ballots can be eliminated.[29]

4. *An Error in the Statement of the General Possibility Theorem*

Blau has pointed out that the General Possibility Theorem is incorrectly stated.[30] The difficulty in the proof arises in attempting to reduce the general problem to the case of three alternatives; specifically, Conditions 2 and 5 were implicitly assumed to hold for the three-member subset mentioned in Condition 1; however, the conditions could hold for a set of alternatives and not for a subset. If Conditions 1 and 2 are replaced by Conditions 1' and 2', Blau shows that the difficulty is avoided, as we have seen in paragraph 4. However, Condition 1' is a strong condition, as the discussion in the text (p. 24) shows.

Murakami [31] suggested as an alternative to the strengthening of Condition 1 a weakening of the definition of a dictator (and thereby a strengthening of the Condition of Nondictatorship). If we introduce

[27] In a subsequent note, May showed that his four conditions were completely independent in the sense that one could find a social decision procedure which satisfied any subset of the conditions and failed to satisfy the others. See "A Note on the Complete Independence of the Conditions for Simple Majority Decision," *Econometrica*, Vol. 21, January, 1953, pp. 172–73. It follows that a possibly useful way to classify social decision procedures is to enumerate which of May's conditions it satisfies.

[28] Y. Murakami, "Some Logical Properties of Arrowian Social Welfare Function," *The Journal of Economic Behavior*, Vol. 1, No. 1, April, 1961, pp. 77–84.

[29] Strictly speaking, this last result has been proved only for the case where no individual is indifferent between any two alternatives.

[30] *Op. cit.* in fn. 18.

[31] Y. Murakami, "A Note on the General Possibility Theorem of the Social Welfare Function," *Econometrica*, Vol. 29, April, 1961, pp. 244–46.

CONDITION 5': *Among the triples of alternatives satisfying Condition* 1, *there is at least one on which no individual is a dictator.*

Then the arguments of paragraph 2, with slight modification, show

THEOREM 3. *Conditions* 1, 3, *P, and* 5' *are inconsistent.*

Condition 5' is a very reasonable extension of the notion of a dictator; to deny it means roughly to say that for every choice on which there can be real disagreement there is a dictator.

III. WHAT IS THE PROBLEM OF SOCIAL CHOICE?

A long series of distinguished critics have argued, in one form or another, that the problem of social choice has been incorrectly posed in this book.[32] I will now argue that these criticisms are based on mis-understandings of my position and indeed of the full implications of the critics' own positive views. Upon close examination, all implicitly accept the essential formulation stated here: The social choice from any given environment is an aggregation of individual preferences. The true grounds for disagreement are the conditions which it is reasonable to impose on the aggregation procedure, and even here it is possible to show that the limits of disagreement are not as wide as might be supposed from some of the more intemperate statements made.

1. *Welfare Judgments*

Bergson's deservedly classic paper of 1938 [33] set the pattern in which most of the subsequent discussion, and in particular my own, has been carried on. It is a refined form of classical utilitarianism, but one which at least faces the problem of commensurating the utilities of different individuals.

[32] See I. M. D. Little, "Social Choice and Individual Values," *Journal of Political Economy,* Vol. 60, October, 1952, pp. 422–32, and "L'avantage collectif," *Économie Appliquée,* Vol. 5, October–December, 1952, pp. 455–68; A. Bergson, "On the Concept of Social Welfare," *Quarterly Journal of Economics,* Vol. 68, May, 1954, pp. 233–52; M. C. Kemp, "Arrow's General Possibility Theorem," *Review of Economic Studies,* Vol. 21, 1953–54, pp. 240–43; J. M. Buchanan, "Individual Choice in Voting and the Market," *Journal of Political Economy,* Vol. 62, August, 1954, pp. 334–43; E. J. Mishan, "An Investigation into Some Alleged Contradictions in Welfare Economics," *Economic Journal,* Vol. 68, September, 1957, pp. 445–54; G. Tullock, Appendix 2 to J. M. Buchanan and G. Tullock, *The Calculus of Consent,* Ann Arbor: The University of Michigan Press, 1962, especially pp. 331–34.

[33] "A Reformulation of Certain Aspects of Welfare Economics," *Quarterly Journal of Economics,* Vol. 52, February, 1938, pp. 310–34.

At the risk of boring the reader with the obvious, let me restate the logic of the welfare judgment, as crystallized in Bergson's formulation. Any social decision has consequences for the individual members of the society. It is first assumed that for each individual there is a way of evaluating these consequences; we do not at the moment specify whether this evaluation is cardinal or ordinal. But so far there are as many evaluations as there are individuals in the society. Classical utilitarianism implicitly and Bergson explicitly call for a second-order evaluation, which I for the moment call a welfare judgment. This is an evaluation of the consequences to all individuals which is based on the evaluations for individuals; specifically, if in each individual valuation, two sets of consequences are indifferent, then the welfare judgment as between the two must also be one of indifference.

The individual values are thus the raw material out of which the welfare judgment is manufactured. As good economists, let us look more closely at the technology of the transformation process and the sensitivity of the output to variations in the inputs.

The collection of welfare judgments on all possible environments is determined by the individual valuation schedules, or individual orderings of social states, to use the terminology of this book. This point is accepted and even urged by Bergson and by Little, although their emphasis sounds very different. They argue that the social welfare function (in Bergson's sense) takes individuals' tastes as given. Given a set of individual orderings, the Bergson procedure is first to associate to each ordering a corresponding utility indicator and then to prescribe a function of the individual utilities whose values serve as an indicator of social welfare. But presumably such a social welfare function could be drawn up for any given set of individual orderings; if we substitute a new set of individual orderings, we have, in Bergson's terminology, a new social welfare function, i.e., a new formula for determining all possible welfare judgments.

This formulation is in no wise different from mine; to each given set of individual orderings is associated a social choice function (see Definition 4, p. 23 of text [34]). It would perhaps have been better for me to use a different term from "social welfare function" for the process of determining a social ordering or choice function from individual orderings, although the difference between Bergson's definition and my own was

[34] The definition cited associates a social ordering with each set of individual orderings; it might have been better to speak more generally of a social choice function and leave for a special assumption the question whether the social choice function should be an ordering. The desirability of the transitivity condition has been criticized and needs discussion: see Section V.

pretty carefully spelled out (p. 23 of text). I will therefore now use the term "constitution," as suggested by Kemp and Asimakopulos.[35] The difference, however, is largely terminological; to have a social welfare function in Bergson's sense, there must be a constitution.[36]

The real point of the Bergson-Little criticisms, then, is not the formulation of the social choice problem as the choice of a constitutuion, but the acceptability of my particular set of conditions. These conditions are of two kinds: those that relate to the social choice function produced by any given set of individual orderings, and those that relate to the way social choices vary with respect to changes in the individual orderings. It is the latter set which are rejected by Bergson and Little. This point was made very clearly by Little: "If tastes change, we may expect a new ordering of all the conceivable states; but we do not require the difference between the new and the old ordering should bear any particular relation to the changes of taste which have occurred. We have, so to speak, a new world and a new order; and we do not demand correspondence between the change in the world and the change in the order." [37]

Just how much weight this point can bear is seen better from the revised set of conditions given in Section II.1 than from the original set. It turns out that there is only one condition which in fact requires a correspondence of the type that Little objects to, the Independence of Irrelevant Alternatives. The area of fundamental disagreement thus narrows down to this one assumption, to be discussed further in Section IV. It should be noted that of the other conditions, two, Collective Rationality and the Pareto principle, are satisfied by Bergson's social welfare function, and the third, Nondictatorship, hardly raises any fundamental questions.

I therefore conclude that the formulation of the social choice problem as the selection of a constitution is not only compatible with the views

[35] M. C. Kemp and A. Asimakopulos, "A Note on 'Social Welfare Functions' and Cardinal Utility," *Canadian Journal of Economics and Political Science*, Vol. 18, May, 1952, pp. 195–200.

[36] A similar failure to appreciate the inescapability of the logical need for a constitution is found in the criticism of M. C. Kemp, *op. cit.*, footnote 32. He argues that the choice of a decision procedure cannot be made except in terms of a particular choice situation, since choice procedures will be evaluated in terms of their consequences. But this argument in no way invalidates the need for a constitution; it says in fact that for each choice situation (or environment), there is an appropriate way of combining individual orderings to arrive at a social decision. This is exactly equivalent to saying that we can combine individual orderings to arrive at a system of welfare judgments sufficient to arrive at a social choice from any environment.

[37] "Social Choice and Individual Values," *op. cit.* in footnote 32, pp. 423–24.

of such critics as Bergson, Little, and Kemp, but in fact is a logical corollary of their positive position.

2. *The Social Decision Process*

Little [38] has argued cogently that a rule for social decision-making is not the same as a welfare judgment. A welfare judgment requires that some one person is judge; a rule for arriving at social decisions may be agreed upon for reasons of convenience and necessity without its outcomes being treated as evaluations by anyone in particular.

This distinction is well taken. I would consider that it is indeed a social decision process with which I am concerned and not, strictly speaking, a welfare judgment by any individual. That said, however, I am bound to add that in my view a social decision process serves as a proper explication for the intuitive idea of social welfare. The classical problems of formulating the social good are indeed of the metaphysical variety which modern positivism finds meaningless; but the underlying issue is real. My own viewpoint towards this and other ethical problems coincides with that expressed by Popper: "Not a few doctrines which are metaphysical, and thus certainly philosophical, can be interpreted as hypostatizations of methodological rules." [39] All the writers from Bergson on agree on avoiding the notion of a social good not defined in terms of the values of individuals. But where Bergson seeks to locate social values in welfare judgments by individuals, I prefer to locate them in the actions taken by society through its rules for making social decisions. This position is a natural extension of the ordinalist view of values; just as it identifies values and choices for the individual, so I regard social values as meaning nothing more than social choices.

In fact, the Bergson formulation cannot be kept distinct from the interpretation of social welfare in terms of social decision processes. In the first place, the argument of paragraph 1 shows that the Bergson social welfare function is necessarily a constitution, that is, a potential social decision process; the body of welfare judgments made by a single individual are determined, in effect, by the social decision process which the individual would have society adopt if he could. In the second place, the location of welfare judgments in any individual, while logically possible, does not appear to be very interesting. "Social welfare" is related to social policy in any sensible interpretation; the welfare judgments formed by any single individual are unconnected with action and therefore sterile. Bergson recognizes the possible difficulty in his 1954

[38] *Ibid.*, p. 427, pp. 430–32.
[39] K. Popper, *The Logic of Scientific Discovery*, New York: Basic Books, 1959, p. 55.

paper; I quote the passage at length since it displays the issue so well.

"I have been assuming that the concern of welfare economics is to counsel individual citizens generally. If a public official is counseled, it is on the same basis as any other citizen. In every instance reference is made to some ethical values which are appropriate for the counseling of the individual in question. In all this I believe I am only expressing the intent of welfare writings generally; or if this is not the intent, I think it should be. But some may be inclined nevertheless to a different conception, which allows still another interpretation of Arrow's theorem. *According to this view the problem is to counsel not citizens generally but public officials* [emphasis added]. Furthermore, the values to be taken as data are not those which might guide the official if he were a private citizen. The official is envisaged instead as more or less neutral ethically. His one aim in life is to implement the values of other citizens as given by some rule of collective decision-making. Arrow's theorem apparently contributes to this sort of welfare economics the negative finding that no consistent social ordering could be found to serve as a criterion of social welfare in the counseling of the official in question." [40]

I need only add that my interpretation of the social choice problem agrees fully with that given by Bergson beginning with the italicized statement.

Where Bergson, Little, and I seek in varying ways to explicate the notion of social welfare in operational terms, Buchanan's positivism is more extreme.[41] Choice is only individual; the very concept of social welfare is inadmissible, and my use of the term "collective rationality" (by which I meant that social choices corresponding to any given set of individual orderings were so interrelated as to satisfy the definition of an ordering) was strongly attacked on the grounds that only individuals can be rational.[42] Nevertheless, Buchanan and Tullock [43] do put great

[40] "On the Concept of Social Welfare," p. 242.

[41] "Individual Choice . . . ," *op. cit.* in fn. 32.

[42] I generally take the view that a definition is a more or less useful convention, no more. But Buchanan and Little both take very seriously the exact words used in the definiendum. Thus, Buchanan does not so much say that collective rationality, as I define it, is an unsatisfactory condition for a constitution as flatly deny that there can be anything called collective rationality. No doubt, words have penumbras of meaning which may not be easy to eliminate in the reader's mind; but this type of confusion seems secondary when explicit definitions are set forth. Buchanan and Little at some points substitute verbal quibblings for genuine argument.

[43] *The Calculus of Consent, op. cit.* in fn. 32, Chapter 6. Since the subsequent references I will make to this work are largely negative, I should note that they do not pertain to the work's essential contribution which is, in my opinion, of major importance.

stress on the selection of a constitution as the central step in developing a social choice mechanism.

3. Welfare Economics, Compensation and Log-Rolling

Unlike the criticisms discussed in the last two paragraphs, which raise important questions of meaning, I feel that those I am about to discuss represent elementary confusions or word play. Little, Bergson, and Mishan all agree that my theorem is not part of welfare economics. Thus, "Arrow's work has no relevance to the traditional theory of welfare economics, which culminates in the Bergson-Samuelson formulation" (Little); "The theorem has little or no bearing on welfare economics" (Bergson).[44] The most obvious remark to be made is that one can hardly think of a less interesting question about my theorem than whether it falls on one side or another of an arbitrary boundary separating intellectual provinces. Since Little and Bergson (and also Samuelson, according to Little) accept the Bergson social welfare function as part of welfare economics, the arguments of the last two paragraphs show that any attempt to divide welfare economics in their sense from the theory of social choice must be artificial. At the very least, welfare economics, no matter how defined, has something to do with the public adoption of economic policy, and it is hard to see how any study of the formation of social decisions can have "no relevance to" or "no bearing on" welfare economics.

A more natural division between welfare economics and the theory of social choice, if there is any point in locating one, is provided by defining the former as the implications of Pareto optimality. I take this to be Mishan's meaning in reading my work out of the honorific domain of welfare economics. In the terms used in this book, instead of seeking a social ordering, we confine ourselves to the unanimity quasi-ordering.

Of course, as has been repeated over and over in the literature, this "new welfare economics" says nothing about choices among Pareto-optimal alternatives.[45] The purpose of the soical welfare function was precisely to extend the unanimity quasi-ordering to a full social ordering.

[44] Little, "Social Choice and Individual Values," p. 425; Bergson, "On the Concept of Social Welfare," p. 243.

[45] This point is made with admirable clarity by R. G. Davis, "Comment on Arrow and the 'New Welfare Economics,'" *Economic Journal*, Vol. 68, December, 1958, pp. 834–35, in a comment on Mishan, *op. cit.* in footnote 32. In effect, Mishan accepted Davis's argument; see "Arrow and the 'New Welfare Economics': A Restatement," *ibid.*, Vol. 68, September, 1958, pp. 595–97. For some odd editorial reason, Mishan's rejoinder to Davis appeared before Davis's note.

The compensation principle, based on the new welfare economics, is not an adequate substitute for a social ordering, as has been shown by Scitovsky, Baumol, and others.[46] However, it has been again used by Buchanan and Tullock in their construction. They very correctly argue that trading of votes on different issues (log-rolling) is essentially equivalent to the payment of compensation, but they fail to recognize the ambiguity of the compensation principle as a social decision process. Tullock goes so far as to state that "in processes in which votes are traded . . . the particular type of irrationality described by Arrow is impossible." [47] He seems to be under the impression that I am describing a procedure for deciding separate issues, without any regard to complementarities and substitutions among them. This is a simple misreading; I am concerned, as are the writers on the compensation principle, with choices among social states; a social state is a whole bundle of issues, and I presupposed that all possible combinations of decisions on the separate issues are considered as alternative social states. That this included log-rolling seemed to me so obvious as not to be worth spelling out. The paradox of social choice cannot be so easily exorcised.[48]

IV. The Independence of Irrelevant Alternatives and Interpersonal Comparisons of Intensity

1. *Ordinalism, Observability, and the Independence of Irrelevant Alternatives*

The essential point of the modern insistence on ordinal utility is the application of Leibniz's principle of the identity of indiscernibles. Only observable differences can be used as a basis for explanation. In the field of consumers' demand theory, the ordinalist position turned out to create no problems; cardinal utility had no explanatory power above and beyond ordinal.

---

[46] T. Scitovsky, "A Note on Welfare Propositions in Economics," *Review of Economic Studies*, Vol. 9, November, 1941, pp. 77–88; W. J. Baumol, "Community Indifference," *ibid.*, Vol. 14, No. 1, 1946–7, pp. 44–48; Chapter IV of the text.

[47] *Op. cit.* in fn. 32, p. 332.

[48] Dahl also notes that an election, in which many issues enter, cannot be interpreted as indicating a majority on any specific issue; he therefore speaks of "minorities" rule as opposed to either majority or minority rule; see *A Preface to Democratic Theory*, Chicago: The University of Chicago Press, 1956, pp. 127–32. However, the significant question is not the existence of a majority on each issue but the existence of a majority on the bundle of issues represented by the candidate over any other attainable bundle.

It is the great merit of Bergson's 1938 paper [49] to have carried the same principle into the analysis of social welfare. The social welfare function was to depend only on indifference maps; in other words, welfare judgments were to be based only on interpersonally observable behavior.

The Condition of Independence of Irrelevant Alternatives extends the requirement of observability one step farther. Given the set of alternatives available for society to choose among, it could be expected that, ideally, one could observe all preferences among the available alternatives, but there would be no way to observe preferences among alternatives not feasible for society.

The austerity imposed by this condition is perhaps stricter than necessary; in many situations, we do have information on preferences for nonfeasible alternatives. It can be argued that, when available, this information should be used in social choice, and some possibilities in this direction will be briefly commented on in the following paragraphs. But clearly, social decision processes which are independent of irrelevant alternatives have a strong practical advantage. After all, every known electoral system satisfies this condition.

It may be worth noting more explicitly than in the text that the market mechanism also operates independently of irrelevant alternatives. If we alter the utility functions of individuals with respect to allocations which are socially infeasible, we do not alter the competitive equilibrium. Indeed, the decentralization of knowledge which is such a virtue of the market mechanism is incompatible with the use of utility comparisons among irrelevant alternatives in arriving at resource allocations.[50]

This paragraph may be concluded by summarizing some conclusions of Guilbaud and Inada, which bring out the underlying meaning of Independence of Irrelevant Alternatives in somewhat different ways. Guilbaud [51] argues that a social welfare function based on individual utilities which are meaningful only up to monotonic transformations

[49] "A Reformulation . . . ," pp. 318–20; see also P. A. Samuelson, *Foundations of Economic Analysis*, Cambridge, Massachusetts: Harvard University Press, 1947, p. 228.

[50] Since the market mechanism does satisfy the Condition of Independence of Irrelevant Alternatives, it must violate another condition, which is clearly that of Collective Rationality (Condition 1 or 1'). This violation is precisely the well-known intersection of community indifference curves. Samuelson's social indifference curves (see P. A. Samuelson, "Social Indifference Curves," *Quarterly Journal of Economics*, Vol. 70, February, 1956, pp. 1–22) satisfy the condition of Collective Rationality but violate that of Independence of Irrelevant Alternatives; the income redistribution associated with each change in social production possibilities requires a high degree of centralization of knowledge about individual utility functions.

[51] *Op. cit.*, pp. 576–84.

must be what is mathematically termed a functional, not a function in the ordinary sense. That is, each social choice must depend on the entire individual ordering. Inada's [52] result is somewhat similar; if the social welfare function is to be determined from individual orderings, then the marginal social rates of substitution among commodity allocations to individuals cannot be determined exclusively from the individuals' marginal rates of substitution at that point; even local social choices must depend upon individual preferences in the large. [53]

2. The Impossibility of Purely Ethical Comparisons

Bergson, in both his papers, takes the position that interpersonal comparisons are purely ethical in nature; this is just another way of saying that only individual indifference maps (and not cardinal utilities) are used in forming welfare judgments. However, especially in his second paper, his exposition brings out the difficulties involved. [54] He comes at points very close to asserting a meaningful empirical interpersonal comparison: "The ultimate criterion would be the perfectly plausible one of the comparative degree to which wants of different orders are satisfied for different individuals. . . . The individual members of the community are all supposed to order social states on the ethical premise that distribution should be according to need." The meaningfulness of "wants of different orders" or of "need" seems to depend on an empirical comparison. But Bergson then veers ? way: "It might even be necessary to pair by separate ethical premises all the indifference curves of each household with all those of every other one." Later, although not necessarily rejecting the existence of meaningful empirical interpersonal comparisons, he reemphasizes that purely ethical comparisons are adequate for the formation of social welfare judgments: "The criterion must be ethical in character. This does not by itself rule out empirical comparability, but it means that even with this supposition one must establish

[52] K. Inada, "On the Economic Welfare Function," Technical Report No. 97, Contract Nonr-225(50) for the Office of Naval Research, Institute for Mathematical Studies in the Social Sciences, Stanford University, Stanford, California, July 13, 1961.

[53] This result presupposes that the social welfare function is defined for all possible utility functions of individuals subject only to the usual conditions of quasi-concavity and monotonicity. If it is known a priori that the utility functions of all individuals are purely individualistic (see Chapter VI) and fall into some very restricted class, such as displaying constant marginal utility for some one commodity, then social welfare functions can be drawn up for which social marginal rates of substitution are completely determined by individual rates at the same point.

[54] "On the Concept of Social Welfare," pp. 244–45.

why the criterion is ethically compelling . . . If one can advance the Utilitarian criterion with empirical comparability then it should also be possible to do so without it." [55]

It seems that the last sentence should almost be inverted. If there is no empirical way of comparing two states (say, indifference curves of two different individuals), there can be no ethical way of distinguishing them. Value judgments may equate empirically distinguishable phenomena, but they cannot differentiate empirically indistinguishable states. The pairing of indifference curves referred to above requires that there be some operational meaning, if only an ideal one, to the comparison.

3. *Interpersonal Comparisons and Enlarged Indifference Maps*

If empirically meaningful interpersonal comparisons have to be based on indifference maps, as we have argued, then the Independence of Irrelevant Alternatives must be violated. The information which enables us to assert that individual A prefers x to y more strongly than B prefers y to x must be based on comparisons by A and B of x and y not only to each other but also to other alternatives.

In fact, the indifference map that must be used will probably contain many more dimensions than might ordinarily be considered. Verbal or other expressive behavior might possibly be added to the economists' more usual comparison of bundles. One cannot help being influenced by such psychological work as that of S. S. Stevens,[55] who could find a cardinal scale for such a phenomenon as pitch by asking subjects which of two reference notes a given note was closer to. The resemblance to (better, identity with) a well-known line of thought, stemming from Pareto, which justifies cardinal utility on the basis of ordinal comparisons of *changes* from one commodity vector to another, is obvious.[57]

The strategy of deriving empirically and then ethically meaningful interpersonal comparisons is apparently to proceed as follows. (1) The preference system of the individual is explored with respect to many irrelevant alternatives, indeed well beyond the regions that are relevant for individual choice. (2) This wider realm of choices can, of course, be

[55] *Ibid.*, pp. 250–51.

[56] S. S. Stevens, "The Psychophysics of Sensory Function," *The American Scientist*, Vol. 48, June, 1961, pp. 226–53; see especially the discussion of alternative scales on pp. 231–33. The method mentioned in the text is referred to by Stevens as a "category scale"; the "magnitude scale," which he prefers, is even more of a break with the typical views of economists on the possibilities of observing behavior.

[57] The classic and still best statement of this position is that of R. Frisch, "Sur un problème d'économie pure," *Norsk Matematisk Forenings Skrifter*, Serie I, No. 16, 1926, pp. 1–40.

represented by utility functions; although these are in principle unique only up to monotonic transformations, in fact a set of utility functions sufficiently restricted to define a cardinal utility appear most natural (as in the use of cardinal utility in explaining risk-taking). (3) Finally, one of the utility differences is widely accepted to have an interpersonal ethical significance and can be used to arrive at the ethical interpersonal equation of utility differences which are not directly comparable.

A simple illustration of the preceding is the suggestion of Dahl [58] that voting and other forms of political activity may be taken as an interpersonal measure of preference intensity. It is assumed, of course, that voting is per se a disutility. Let x and y be two alternative social states, let v be the act of voting, and let (x, v) be the combination of the social state x and the act of voting. If an individual prefers (x, v) to y, then his preference for x over y must be at least sufficiently great to cover the disutility of voting. We can find a family of utility indicators in the joint space of social states and the act of voting. Suppose in particular we can find one utility indicator for which the social state and the act of voting are independent, i.e., the utilities of the two are additive. Then to say that (x, v) is preferred to y is to say that

$$U(x) - c(v) > U(y),$$

where U is the utility ascribed to a social state, and $c(v)$ is the disutility ascribed to voting. Equivalently, we can say that

$$U(x) - U(y) > c(v).$$

If finally we make the ethical assumption that the disutility of voting is equivalent for all individuals, then the utility differences between x and y for all those voting for x can be assumed at least equal to the disutility of voting and vice versa.

Unfortunately, most of the links in this chain are weak. In the first place, all that can be established about a utility difference is an inequality; we know that the utility difference of one who votes for x is at least the disutility of voting, but it might be a good deal more. Hence, counting the votes is not sufficient to find the sum of the utilities. Nor is this problem peculiar to this example; it is intrinsic in the mechanism of political choice.

Second, the ethical assumption of interpersonal equality of the disutility of voting is not one which we would really insist on; the disutility of voting might be expected to differ among individuals depending on wealth or intelligence or health.

[58] *Op. cit.*, pp. 134–5.

Third, even with all the strong assumptions that have been made, the problems raised by not requiring the Independence of Irrelevant Alternatives occur. If the voting actually takes place, then the disutility of voting has been incurred and has partially wiped out for the winners their gain in the victory of x; at the same time those losers who felt strongly enough to vote for y have not only suffered the social acceptance of x but also the disutility of voting. Thus if x is chosen as the result of voting, it could easily happen that the sum of utilities of the entire process, including the act of voting, be less than if y were imposed without voting.

Of course, the best solution of all, according to this logic, would be to impose x without voting. This indeed would be the true meaning of using irrelevant alternatives as a measure of preference intensities; it is the willingness to incur the sacrifice of voting, not the sacrifice itself, which is the measure of intensity. But how can this be made operational?

Basically, I can only leave the matter with this conundrum. But in the next two paragraphs two particular classes of interpersonal comparisons based on enlarged indifference maps will be discussed.

4. *Extended Sympathy* [59]

One type of interpersonal comparison to be found in the most ancient ethical writings has yet to receive significant expression and formalization in political and economic contexts. It is exemplified, in perhaps an extreme form, by an inscription supposedly found in an English graveyard.

> Here lies Martin Engelbrodde,
> Ha'e mercy on my soul, Lord God,
> As I would do were I Lord God,
> And Thou wert Martin Engelbrodde.

People seem prepared to make comparisons of the form: State x is better (or worse) for me than state y is for you.[60] This is certainly one way of approaching the notion of an appropriate income distribution; if I am richer than you, I may find it easy to make the judgment that it is better for you to have the marginal dollar than for me.

---

[59] I am indebted to H. K. Zassenhaus for stressing to me the importance of this notion for welfare judgments.

[60] A more formal presentation of this notion is given by my colleague, P. Suppes, "Two Formal Models for Moral Principles," Technical Report No. 15, Office of Naval Research Contract Nonr 225(17), Applied Mathematics and Statistics Laboratory, Stanford University, Stanford, California, November 1, 1957, pp. 17–18.

The ordinalist would ask what possible meaning the comparison could have to anyone; a comparison should represent at least a conceivable choice among alternative actions. Interpersonal comparisons of the extended sympathy type can be put in operational form; the judgment takes the form: It is better (in my judgment) to be myself in state x than to be you in state y.

In this form, the characteristics that define an individual are included in the comparison. In effect, these characteristics are put on a par with the items usually regarded as constituting an individual's wealth. The possession of tools would ordinarily be regarded as part of the social state; why not the possession of the skills to use the tools and the intelligence which lies behind those skills? Individuals, in appraising each other's states of well-being, consider not only material possessions but also find themselves "desiring this man's scope and that man's art." [61]

The principle of extended sympathy as a basis for interpersonal comparisons seems basic to many of the welfare judgments made in ordinary practice. But it is not easy to see how to construct a theory of social choice from this principle.

5. The Ability to Discriminate

A recurrent approach to interpersonal comparisons has been the use of just noticeable utility differences as interpersonally valid units.[62] The clearest discussion, which will be analyzed here, is that of Goodman and Markowitz. They argue that no individual can make indefinitely fine comparisons of alternatives. Hence, it may be supposed that each individual has only a finite number of levels of discrimination; a change from one level to the next represents the minimum difference which is discernible to an individual. Goodman and Markowitz then make the basic ethical assumption that the significance of a change from one discretion level to the next is the same for all individuals and independent of the level from which the change is made.

---

[61] For an interesting discussion of the moral implications of the position that many attributes of the individual are similar in nature to external possessions, see V. C. Walsh, *Scarcity and Evil*, Englewood Cliffs, New Jersey: Prentice-Hall, 1961. I am indebted for this reference to R. A. Mundell.

[62] See the discussion of Borda in Part I, p. 99; F. Y. Edgeworth, *Mathematical Psychics*, London: C. Kegan and Paul, 1881, pp. 7-8; W. E. Armstrong, "Utility and the Theory of Welfare," *Oxford Economics Papers*, New Series, Vol. 3, October, 1951, pp. 259-71; and L. Goodman and H. Markowitz, *op. cit.*, fn. 14. For excellent analyses of Armstrong's and Goodman-Markowitz's views, see Rothenberg (*op. cit.* in fn. 7), Chapters 7 and 8.

The consequence of this assumption (in conjunction with other, more usual, conditions, Collective Rationality, the Pareto principle, and Equality) is that social choice is made according to a sum of individual utilities, where the utility of any individual for any social state is the number of discrimination levels below the level in which the individual places the given social state.

Two problems are raised by this procedure: one is the operational meaning of the discrimination levels and the other is the ethical desirability of using discrimination levels as an interpersonal measure. In regard to the first, it must be asked what experiments could one conduct, at least ideally, which would define the discrimination level to be attached to any social alternative by any individual? Actually, Goodman and Markowitz do not give a clear account. They distinguish [63] between knowing the true discrimination level l_{ij} of the alternative j for the individual i and the ranking a_j of that alternative among a fixed set of alternatives. They suggest that only the latter are observable and should or could be used. The implied experiment can be stated as follows: There is a subset S of all logically possible social states such that every environment (set of actually attainable social states) which is at all likely to occur will be a subset of S. Each individual then draws his indifference map within S; by the assumption of finite discriminatory ability, he will simply divide S into a finite number of subsets within each of which he is completely indifferent. These subsets are then assigned ranks, which are the utilities.

The ranks can, however, easily depend on the choice of S. Suppose, for example, that a new commodity becomes available but is prohibitively expensive. If S is expanded by adding distributions of commodities including the new one, it may contain elements more desirable than any of the old ones, as well as some less desirable than some old ones. The additional components of the social state vector will increase the possibility of discrimination, so that it is to be expected that the enlargement of S will introduce new discrimination levels whose ranks lie between some of the old ones. Then the perceived ranks, a_{ij}, of the original alternatives will be altered by the introduction of new alternatives which may not be technologically feasible.

This objection is, of course, simply another illustration of the argument for the principle of Independence of Irrelevant Alternatives.

The ethical desirability of basing welfare judgments on discrimination levels can be examined best by means of an illustration. Since the fundamental function of any theory of social welfare is to supply criteria for income distribution, let us assume the existence of a single commodity

[63] *Op. cit.*, pp. 5–6.

(income) to be distributed between two individuals; the total quantity of the commodity will be taken as 1. Let x be the amount given to individual 1, $1 - x$ the amount given to individual 2. According to Goodman and Markowitz, x is chosen to maximize $U_1(x) + U_2(1 - x)$, where the functions U_i represent the discrimination levels of the two individuals.

Each individual could receive from 0 to 1 unit, but because of his finite discriminatory ability this interval is divided into a finite number of segments, within each of which the individual cannot discriminate. Suppose then individual 1 divides the interval into m equal parts, within each of which he is indifferent; for definiteness, suppose that each part includes its lower limit and excludes its upper. The amount 1 is in a class by itself. The utility function for individual 1 is then

$$U_1(x) = [mx],$$

where $[y]$ means the largest integer not exceeding y. Similarly, if individual 2 divides the interval from 0 to 1 into n parts, his utility function is

$$U_2(1 - x) = [n(1 - x)].$$

Suppose now the $n > m$, i.e., individual 2 is capable of finer discrimination than individual 1. Then the Goodman-Markowitz criterion yields the remarkable conclusion that the entire income should go to individual 2. For suppose that $x > 0$ at the optimum. Then $U_1(x) \geq 0$. If $U_1(x) > 0$, let

$$U_1(x) = r.$$

Then

$$mx \geq [mx] = U_1(x) = r,$$

so that

$$U_2(1 - x) = [n(1 - x)] \leq \left[n - r\left(\frac{n}{m}\right) \right].$$

Since $n > m$ and $r > 0$,

$$n - r\left(\frac{n}{m}\right) < n - r,$$

and since the right-hand side is an integer,

$$U_2(1 - x) \leq \left[n - r\left(\frac{n}{m}\right) \right] < n - r = n - U_1(x),$$

or

$$U_1(x) + U_2(1 - x) < n.$$

On the other hand, if $x = 0$, $1 - x = 1$, we have

$$U_1(0) + U_2(1) = [0] + [n] = n > U_1(x) + U_2(1 - x),$$

which contradicts the presumed optimality of $x > 0$, provided $U_1(x) > 0$. If $x > 0$, but $U_1(x) = 0$, note that

$$U_1(x) + U_2(1 - x) = 0 + [n(1 - x)] < n = U_1(0) + U_2(1),$$

so that the same contradiction holds.[64]

That a slight difference in sensitivity should lead to complete inequality hardly seems ethically reasonable.[65]

V. COLLECTIVE RATIONALITY

The condition that welfare judgments should take the form of an ordering has been much less disputed than others, although Buchanan (see Section III.3) argues that rationality is a property of individuals only and there is no reason to attribute rationality to society. There have been other incidental comments (e.g., by Kemp [66]) that a social decision process might well sacrifice transitivity if necessary to satisfy other conditions.

The two properties which characterize an ordering are connectedness and transitivity (see p. 13 of text). Connectedness, when understood, can hardly be denied; it simply requires that some social choice be made from any environment. Abstention from a decision cannot exist; some social state will prevail.

[64] This result is obviously closely related to the discussion of J. von Neumann and O. Morgenstern of games with discrete utility scales; there too the less discerning player is completely discriminated against. See *Theory of Games and Economic Behavior*, second edition, Princeton, New Jersey: Princeton University Press, 1947, pp. 614-16.

[65] Examples such as the above may be more convincing than they should be, because of hidden empirical content. If in fact we never run across two individuals related as above, then our intuitive rejection of the completely unequal income distribution may be incorrect; our intuition is guided by situations we have encountered, and it could be that if we were to meet two individuals, one of whom is more sensitive than the other, no matter what their income levels are, we would accept the Goodman-Markowitz solution. Goodman and Markowitz have suggested to me orally that in fact discrimination levels would become closer together at lower levels of income (this is one interpretation of diminishing marginal utility of income); thus, the sum of utilities would be maximized at some point short of complete inequality. Since in realistic cases, it could be argued, the Goodman-Markowitz social welfare function does not lead to blatant absurdity, we should not use the evidence of the example in the text. Actually, it would not be difficult to construct examples similar to the one in the text for which, however, increasing ability to discriminate at lower levels of income is sufficient to prevent complete inequality, but nevertheless a moderate difference in the number of levels of discrimination leads to a very great inequality of income.

[66] *Op. cit.* in fn. 32, pp. 242-43.

However, it cannot be denied that there is an important sense in which one may speak, although loosely, of the absence of decision. In any historically given situation there is a social state which has a preferred status in social choice in that it will be adopted in the absence of a specific decision to the contrary. Politically, the status quo has this property, as is frequently all too obvious. If one considers the entire distribution of goods, the preferred alternative is slightly different. Suppose that social state x obtains when the environment is S. Now suppose there is an innovation, so that the environment expands. In a basically free enterprise economy there will be an adaptation which is controlled by property laws and the workings of the system. The resulting social state, say x^1, which in general differs from x, will automatically prevail unless there is a specific legislative decision to alter it.

There is a fundamental divergence of opinion, which has not been fully recognized, on whether or not social choices should be historically conditioned, or, equivalently, whether or not inaction is an alternative different from other alternatives.[67] The social welfare function approach, whether in Bergson's version or in mine, and "populistic democracy," as Dahl[68] terms it, both imply that the social choice at any moment is determined by the range of alternative social states available (given the preferences of individuals); there is no special role given to one alternative because it happens to be identical to or derived from a historically given one. In the case of choice between two alternatives, this point of view tends toward majority rule.[69]

Buchanan and Tullock, on the other hand, distinguish between retaining and changing the status quo most clearly in the following quotation:[70] "We must sharply differentiate between two kinds of decisions: (1) the positive decision that authorizes action for the social group, and (2) the negative decision that effectively blocks action proposed by another group. If a group is empowered to make decisions resulting in positive action by/for the whole group, we shall say that this group effectively 'rules' for the decisions in question. It does not seem meaningful to say

[67] The sharpest confrontation of opposing views is found in the controversy between A. Downs, "In Defense of Majority Voting," *Journal of Political Economy*, Vol. 69, April, 1961, pp. 192–99, and G. Tullock, "Reply to a Traditionalist," *ibid.*, pp. 200–03.

[68] See Dahl, *op. cit.*, Chapter 2, especially p. 41.

[69] The refusal to consider any alternative as being preferred on historical grounds removes one reason for nonneutrality (see Section II.3) and hence, according to May's argument, implies majority rule if his other, less controversial, conditions are accepted. However, there may be other reasons for rejecting neutrality in specific situations, so that qualified majorities may still be called for.

[70] *Op. cit.*, pp. 258–59.

that the power to block action constitutes effective 'rule.' . . . The power of blocking action is not what we normally mean, or should mean, when we speak of 'majority rule' or 'minority rule.' " The asymmetry between action and inaction is closely related to their support of unanimity as the ideal criterion of choice; [71] under such a rule, the status quo is a highly privileged alternative.

It is against this background that the importance of the transitivity condition becomes clear. Those familiar with the integrability controversy in the field of consumer's demand theory [72] will observe that the basic problem is the same: the independence of the final choice from the path to it. Transitivity will insure this independence; from any environment, there will be a chosen alternative, and, in the absence of a deadlock, no place for the historically given alternative to be chosen by default.

That an intransitive social choice mechanism may as a matter of observed fact produce decisions that are clearly unsatisfactory has been brought out in different ways by Riker [73] and by Dahl. [74] Riker's emphasis is on the possibility that legislative rules may lead to choice of a proposal opposed by a majority, Dahl's rather on the possibility that the rules lead to a deadlock and therefore a socially undesired inaction. The notion of a "democratic paralysis," a failure to act due not to a desire for inaction but an inability to agree on the proper action, seems to me to deserve much further empirical, as well as theoretical, study.

Collective rationality in the social choice mechanism is not then merely an illegitimate transfer from the individual to society, but an important attribute of a genuinely democratic system capable of full adaptation to varying environments.

[71] In the absence of costs of decision-making; it is only these costs which, in their theory, explain the acceptance of less-than-unanimous decisions.

[72] See footnote 5, p. 13 of text. Since the writing of the text, several important papers have been written in this area; see H. Houthakker, "Revealed Preference and the Utility Function," *Economica*, New Series, Vol. 17, May, 1950, pp. 159-74; H. Uzawa, "Preference and Rational Choice in the Theory of Consumption," Chapter 9 in K. J. Arrow, S. Karlin, and P. Suppes (eds.), *Mathematical Methods in the Social Sciences, 1959*, Stanford, California: Stanford University Press, 1960. Ville's paper has been translated by P. K. Newman as "The Existence-Conditions of a Total Utility Function," *Review of Economic Studies*, Vol. 19, No. 2, 1951–52, pp. 123–128. An excellent historical survey has been given by P. A. Samuelson, "The Problem of Integrability in Utility Theory," *Economica*, Vol. 17, November, 1950, pp. 355–85.

[73] W. H. Riker, "The Paradox of Voting and Congressional Rules for Voting on Amendments," *American Political Science Review*, Vol. 52, June, 1958, pp. 349–66.

[74] *Op. cit.*, pp. 39–41.

INDEX

COWLES FOUNDATION MONOGRAPHS

1. Charles F. Roos, *Dynamic Economics* (out of print)
2. Charles F. Roos, *NRA Economic Planning* (out of print)
3. Alfred Cowles and Associates, *Common-Stock Indexes* (2d edition)
4. Dickson H. Leavens, *Silver Money* (out of print)
5. Gerhard Tintner, *The Variate Difference Method* (out of print)
6. Harold T. Davis, *The Analysis of Economic Time Series* (out of print)
7. Jacob L. Mosak, *General Equilibrium Theory in International Trade* (out of print)
8. Oscar Lange, *Price Flexibility and Employment*
9. George Katona, *Price Control and Business* (out of print)
10. Tjalling C. Koopmans, ed., *Statistical Inference in Dynamic Economic Models*
11. Lawrence R. Klein, *Economic Fluctuations in the United States, 1921-1941* (out of print)
12. Kenneth J. Arrow, *Social Choice and Individual Values* (2d edition)
13. Tjalling C. Koopmans, ed., *Activity Analysis of Production and Allocation*
14. William C. Hood and Tjalling C. Koopmans, eds., *Studies in Econometric Method*
15. Clifford Hildreth and F. G. Jarrett, *A Statistical Study of Livestock Production and Marketing*
16. Harry M. Markowitz, *Portfolio Selection: Efficient Diversification of Investments*
17. Gerard Debreu, *Theory of Value: An Axiomatic Analysis of Economic Equilibrium*
18. Alan S. Manne and Harry M. Markowitz, eds., *Studies in Process Analysis: Economy-Wide Production Capabilities*
19. Donald D. Hester and James Tobin, eds., *Risk Aversion and Portfolio Choice*
20. Donald D. Hester and James Tobin, eds., *Studies of Portfolio Behavior*
21. Donald D. Hester and James Tobin, eds., *Financial Markets and Economic Activity*